Nuggets
of
Gold

Nuggets of Gold

From each book of the Old Testament

Genesis through Malachi

Selection of Bible Passages and Comments by

Clay T Buckingham
Major General, US Army (retired)

For family and friends

October 2011
(republished July 2015)

All Bible passages are taken from the New International Version
except where indicated.

*"Thy Word is a lamp unto my feet
and a light unto my path."*
(Psalms 119:105 KJV)

Nuggets of Gold
By Clay T. Buckingham,
Major General, US Army (retired)

Copyright © 2015 by Clay T. Buckingham
(Original publication: 2011)

ISBN-13: 978-1514626672

ISBN-10: 1514626675

Index

Introduction

Dear Family and Friends

Several years ago Clara and I started reading through the Old Testament again. This time we decided to identify a few passages from each book which seemed to have particular relevance for today. Shortly after we started, it became clear that everything was relevant in one way or another. This made it necessary to be very selective. For every passage chosen, we found many, many other passages just as relevant.

As we proceeded, I decided to write some comments on each passage selected. This led to the idea of sending these passages and comments out to our immediate family and some close friends, which we did, starting in 2006. We felt like we were digging for nuggets in an endless gold mine so we started using the title, *Nuggets of Gold*. It has taken over six years to complete the project.

It may seem presumptuous that a layman with no formal theological training would attempt an exegesis of this scope. My credentials are that during the past 65 years, since deciding to follow Jesus, I have participated in over 2,000 small group Bible study sessions, mostly under the auspices of the Officers' Christian Fellowship of the USA. I have also been privileged to sit under the preaching and teaching of hundreds of the most godly and effective preachers and Bible teachers of this era, both in military chapels, civilian churches, and at OCF conferences and conference centers. But probably the best preparation for this task has been a lifetime of personal reading, studying, memorizing and meditating on the Word of God. *"The entrance of thy Word brings light. It brings understanding to the simple"* (Psalm 119:130).

So why did we choose the Old Testament and not the New Testament? The reason is simply that the Old Testament was written first, and lays the groundwork for the New Testament. The writers of the New Testament, which is all about Jesus, were all Jews, steeped in Jewish history and traditions. They had a thorough knowledge and understanding of the Hebrew Scriptures. They frequently referred to the Old Testament as they wrote the New Testament books. The roots of the New Testament are deeply embedded in the Old Testament. It is impossible to understand the New Testament without a working knowledge of the Old Testament.

Reading through the Old Testament leaves one with a sense of anticipation that there is more to come. The Old Testament is not the end of the story. The New Testament is the continuation of the Old Testament. Neither is complete without the other. The New Testament is 'the rest of the story.'

"And this is the testimony (of the New Testament). God has given us eternal life, and this life is in His Son (Jesus Christ). He who has the Son has life; he who does not have the Son of God does NOT have life" (1 John 5:11-12).

"... But these (the New Testament scriptures) are written that you may believe that Jesus is the Christ, the Son of God, and that by believing you may have life in His name" (John 20:30-31).

Although I am the author of the comments in *Nuggets of Gold*, Clara has read them thoroughly and made many helpful suggestions in content, syntax and grammar. She has also provided comprehensive and skillful editing. So this really has been a joint project.

A final note: some of the views expressed in the following pages are controversial and non-traditional. They are my own interpretations of the meaning and application of the biblical texts, and I take full responsibility for these views. Whether you agree with them or not, hopefully they will cause you to think deeply and critically about your own convictions.

Gold mining in the Old Testament has given me a wonderfully new and refreshing sense of my Jewish heritage as a believer and follower of Jesus the Messiah, the Christ, the Son of God, my Savior and my Lord.

Clay Buckingham

Nuggets of Gold

Genesis

Genesis - from the Greek 'to be born'. The origin or coming into being of something. Similar words -- generate (to begin); generator (a machine which produces - begins - electricity), regenerate (to begin again), genetics (having to do with beginnings of life). The book of Genesis is God's explanation of the origin, the beginning, of everything - the universe, the earth, plant life, animal life, human life.

It All Began With God. Genesis 1:1. *"In the beginning, God ..."* This is the fundamental cornerstone of faith. If I understand and firmly hold that God was *in the beginning*, then the whole of the Christian faith makes ultimate sense, and life has purpose. If I do not, then life has no purpose and I am lost, thrashing about in meaningless intellectual and moral chaos.

God Created. Genesis 1:1. *"In the beginning, God created ..."* There is no other viable explanation. Evolutionists can go back in logic just so far, but they cannot explain from their theory how life actually started. To suggest that life just somehow emerged out of primordial slime is simply a senseless, wild guess. To believe the Scripture, that *"... in Him was life ..." (John 1:4)* makes ultimate sense and is the foundation for hope, joy, understanding, wisdom, compassion, purpose, service, fellowship and peace.

Man Is The Image Of God. Genesis 1: 27. *"So God created man in His own image, in the image of God He created him; male and female He created them."* God created mankind in His image -- in His likeness. He created them male and female. Therefore, God has both a male and female nature, since both men and women are made in the image of God. Men and women also have equal value in the sight of God. God has assigned different roles to men and women, both in procreation and in the family and church structure, but throughout Scripture, God upholds the essential equal worth of both men and women.

Woman As Man's Companion And Helper. Genesis 2:18. *"The Lord God said, 'It is not good for the man to be alone. I will make a helper suitable for him.'"* The primary role of a woman in marriage is to be the companion and helper of her husband. She is to be there for him physically, emotionally, intellectually, spiritually, and sexually. He should never feel that she has left him alone - to function by himself - in any of these areas. She is to help him, in every appropriate way: in his profession; in his ministry; in his home life; in his health; and in his personal walk with the Lord. He should know that she is always there for him and that he and she are living every aspect of their marriage together.

Created With Sexuality. Genesis 6:2. *"The sons of God saw that the daughters of men were beautiful, and they married ... them ..."* Men are naturally attracted to women. God made men that way. By the time a girl is in her mid-teens, she has become a lightning rod for men of all ages. Girls need to understand this and develop a strong 'sales resistance' toward all men. Men should understand this, keep their distance, and save for marriage the consummation of this attraction. Also, women do not need to decorate their faces or expose their bodies in order to attract men. Men are attracted to them by nature.

Living Responsibly. Genesis 4:9-10 and 9:5. *Then the Lord said to Cain, 'Where is your brother Abel?" "I don't know." he replied, "Am I my brother's keeper?" The Lord said, "What have you done? Listen. Your brother's blood cries out to me from out of the ground."... "From each man I will demand an accounting for the life of his fellow man."* Yes, we are accountable, in some way or another, for every person who comes into our lives. Jesus said, *"... and the (second greatest Commandment) is to love your neighbor as yourself."* Reach out and hold on to the people around you. Both you and your friends will be steadied, strengthened, and encouraged. We can all make it if we hold on to each other.

Get Moving. Genesis 12:1. *"The Lord said to Abram, 'Leave your country, your people and your father's household and go to the place I will show you.'"* Leave and Go. This is one of the most compelling of God's truths. We are to get up and leave what God tells us to leave and go where He tells us to go. This is true obedience. It starts in the mind and then spreads out to all of life.

God says, Repent, which means Turn Around.
-- Leave sin. Turn to righteous living.
-- Leave your old life. Turn to the new life in Jesus.
-- Leave doubt. Turn to faith.
-- Leave despair. Turn to hope.
-- Leave bitterness. Turn to forgiveness.
-- Leave fear. Turn to confidence.
-- Leave anxiety. Turn to peace.
-- Leave evil Imaginations. Turn to the mind of Christ.
-- Leave idleness. Turn to useful activity.

-- Leave self. Turn to service of others.
-- Leave getting. Turn to giving.
Now Get moving!

Believe God. Genesis 15:6. *"Abram believed God ..."* To believe God is the essence of faith. The question is not, "Do I believe *in* God." The question is, "Do I *believe* God." God has spoken to us through His Word -- the Bible. Do you believe God when He says? --

"For all have sinned and come short of the glory of God."
"The wages of sin is death."
"Your sins have separated you from God."
"Jesus died for our sins."
"The blood of Jesus Christ cleanses us of all sin."
"If we confess our sins, He is faithful and just to forgive us our sins and to cleanse us from all unrighteousness."
"God has given us eternal life and this life is in His Son. He who has the Son has life. He who does not have the Son of God does not have life."

Peter said, *"To whom shall we go? You (Jesus) have the words of eternal life.'"*
Paul said, *"For I believed God that it would be done exactly as it was told me."*

To believe God is authentic faith.

Exodus

Exodus - Webster's definition: 'a mass departure'. Biblically, the mass departure of the Israelites out of Egypt and eventually into the Promised Land. Out of somewhere into somewhere. They didn't simply leave Egypt. They were headed somewhere - toward the Promised Land. God never directs us just to move out of something or somewhere. He always directs us to move out of somewhere in order that we might move into somewhere else. There is always a destination involved with God's command to move. Don't move out of your college or work situation or place of residence until it is very clear to you where or what God wants you to move into.

A Time for Prayer, And A Time For Action. Exodus 14:15. *"Then the Lord said to Moses, 'Why are you crying out to me? Tell the Israelites to move on.'"* The *Living Bible* paraphrases this as God saying to Moses, *"Quit praying and forward march."* Praying is not enough. Praying and planning is not enough. The whole formula is "Pray, then Plan, then Act." You are at a crossroads. It's a big decision. Pray for wisdom. Then devise a plan. Use the wisdom received from God to inform and temper your own God given analytical ability. Make a decision. Then act. Get up and move out. Forward march! Put your shoulder to the plow and push. Exert physical and mental energy. Work up a real sweat. Keep going. Don't look back. Never let your lazy body and wandering mind convince you that prayer and planning can substitute for physical and intellectual action. It cannot. But also don't forget that prayer and planning come first - in that order. Pray. Plan. Act.

The Ten Commandments. Exodus 20:1-17. *"And God spoke all these words ..."* Read them once a month. Commit them to memory. They are the main framework of Western law. They have universal application, regardless of culture, race, language, or religion. Judge every 'thought, word and deed' by the First Commandment. Am I putting other gods before the God of the whole universe, the Creator of Heaven and Earth? What 'other gods'? The god of acceptance by my peers? The god of pleasure, the god of ambition, the god of achievement, the god of money, the god of personal appearance, the god of possessions, the god of prestige, the god of fame, the god of promotion, the god of self-interest?

God Is With You. Exodus 23:20. *"See, I am sending an angel ahead of you to guard you along the way and to bring you to the place I have prepared."* This is another major theme of Scripture. Am I ever really alone? Never. Not for the Christian anyway. Why? Because the Christian has asked Jesus Christ to take up residence in his heart (mind, soul, spirit). Heading out on a dangerous trip? Facing a difficult decision? Making a major change? Suffering from a serious illness? Grieving the loss of something or someone very precious to you? Claim Exodus 23:20 for yourself. *"See, I am sending an angel ahead of you to guard you along the way and to bring you to the place I have prepared."*

Conversation With God. Exodus 33:12,14-15,17,19, 21.   How is your conversation with God? Is it face to face, back and forth? Consider the conversational interaction in these verses: *"Moses said to the Lord ... The Lord replied ... Then Moses said ... And the Lord said ... Then Moses said ... And the Lord said ..."* Is your dialogue with God as intimate and explicit as this? We often hear people say, "You must 'walk the walk' as well as 'talk the talk.'" True. But our walk with God will be only aimless wandering unless we also 'talk' with God. We must 'talk the walk' with God before we can truly 'walk the walk' before people.

Ambassadors for Christ. Exodus 35:1. *"Moses assembled the whole Israelite community and said to them, 'These are the things the Lord has commanded you to do.'"* An ambassador from nation A to nation B represents truthfully to the government of nation B the policies and positions of the government of nation A. Here Moses was truthfully telling the people of Israel the instructions he had received from God. Moses was a good ambassador of God. In 2 Corinthians 5:20, Paul says, *"We are therefore Christ's ambassadors' as though God were making His appeal through us."* Am I truthfully, as a good ambassador, representing Jesus Christ - His teachings, His way of life - to the people around me?

Earning God's Blessings. Exodus 39:42-43. *"The Israelites had done all the work just as the Lord had commanded Moses. Moses inspected the work and saw that they had done it just as the Lord had commanded. So Moses blessed them."* Do you want the commendation of your superior? Then do what he told you to do exactly as he told you to do it. Does a subordinate (or your child) carry out your instructions exactly as you gave them to him? Then give him your blessing. Do you want the blessing of God? Then do exactly as He commands you.

Leviticus

Sinning Unintentionally. Leviticus 4:13, 4:32, 5:17. *"If the whole Israelite community sins unintentionally and does what is forbidden in any of the Lord's commands, even though the community is unaware of the matter, they are guilty ... When a leader sins unintentionally and does what is forbidden in any of the commands of the Lord, he is guilty ... If one person sins and does what is forbidden in any of the Lord's commands even though he does not know it, he is guilty and will be held responsible."* Ignorance of the law is no excuse. God states that if a nation, leader, or individual sins unintentionally, that nation, leader or individual is still guilty and will be held responsible. We should learn what God commands and then do it. And also, ask forgiveness for unintentional sins, as King David did.

Making Restitution. Leviticus 6: 1-5. *"The Lord said to Moses: 'If anyone sins and is unfaithful to the Lord by deceiving his neighbor about something entrusted to him, or left in his care, or stolen, or if he cheats him, or if he finds lost property and lies about it, or if he swears falsely, or if he commits any such sin that people may do -- when he thus sins and becomes guilty, he must return what he has stolen or taken by extortion or what was entrusted to him, or the lost property found, or whatever it was he swore falsely about. He must make restitution in full, add a fifth of the value to it and give it all to the owner ...'"* In addition to confession of sin and repentance, God requires restitution -- full and with interest. A man who has robbed a bank, who confesses and repents (promises God he will never do it again), must still pay the money back to the bank. If I sin against my wife or children or friends, I must not only confess it to God and repent of ever doing the same thing again, but I must in some way make restitution to the person sinned against. For instance, if I have unfairly denigrated a friend in front of others and God reveals to me that I did so unfairly, then in addition to confession and repentance before God, I must publicly confess that my words were unfair, and apologize to the individual defamed. However, if I have denigrated my friend *in my heart only* I do **not** need to go to him and apologize for something he knows nothing about. But, in the spirit of restitution, I do need to consider his positive accomplishments and publicly give him credit for these.

Numbers

Honor God. Numbers 25:12-13. *"...I am making my covenant of peace with him ... because he was zealous for the honor of his God..."* Do you want peace with God? Be zealous -- work hard -- for His honor (His praise, His glory). Do everything for the enhancement of the reputation of God among your friends and associates...and receive His peace (His blessings) upon you.

Keeping My Promises. Numbers 30: 1-2. *"This is what the Lord commands: 'When a man makes a vow to the Lord or...obligates himself by a pledge, he must not break his word but must do everything he said.'"* Am I a person of my word? If I promise to do something, can people count on me to do it? If I say that I will meet you at 10:30 AM will I be there? Or will I be late? Or not show up at all. If at the wedding alter I 'pledge my troth' to my bride to 'love, honor and keep her until death do us part,' will she know (because she has witnessed my life of integrity) that I will still be keeping this promise fifty years from now?

Trying To Hide Sins. Numbers 32:23. *"...you may be sure that your sin will find you out."* Regardless of how we try, we cannot hide from God. Jonah tried, and failed. Sins done even in private will eventually become public knowledge. Lesson: Don't do anything you don't want others to find out about because eventually they will.

Deuteronomy

Deuteronomy - *Deuter* (second) + *nomos* (law). The idea is that Deuteronomy contains the second part of God's law. Exodus and Leviticus contain the first part. The 'Law' is God's instructions for living productively. "When all else fails, read the instructions."

Follow The Rules. Deuteronomy 4:1-2. *"Hear now, O Israel, the decrees and laws I am about to teach you. Follow them so that you may live and may go in and take possession of all that the Lord, the God of your fathers, is giving you."* The law was given for our own good, not to keep us from having fun. The Law was given so that we might live productive, contributing, significant, joyful, fulfilled lives. Jesus said, *"I am come that they might have life, and that they might have it more abundantly."*

Deuteronomy 4:40. *"Keep His decrees and commands so that it may go well with you and your children."*

Deuteronomy 5:33. *"Walk in all the ways the Lord your God has commanded you so that you may live and prosper..."*

Deuteronomy 6:3. *"Hear, O Israel, and be careful to obey so that it may go well with you and that you may increase greatly."*

Deuteronomy 6:18. *Do what is right and good in the Lord's sight so that it may go well with you..."*

Deuteronomy 6:24. *"The Lord commanded us to obey all these decrees and to fear the Lord our God so that we might always prosper and be kept alive..."*

Deuteronomy 7:13. *"If you pay attention to these laws and are careful to follow them, then the Lord your God will... love you and bless you..."*

Deuteronomy 8:1. *"Be careful to follow every command I have given you so that you might live and increase..."*

It Is All For Your Own Good. Deuteronomy 10:12-13. *"And now, O Israel, what does the Lord ask of you but to fear the Lord your God, to walk in all His ways, to love Him, to serve the Lord your God with all your heart and soul, and to observe* *the Lord's commands and decrees that I am giving you today for your own good."* Who would really enjoy playing tennis or basketball or soccer if there were no rules or boundaries? How tragic to grow up in a family where there are no firm rules or boundaries. How futile to try to live happily without rules or boundaries. We are to "observe *the Lord's 'rules and boundaries'... for our own good."* And life is so much more fun lived His way.

Seek Him And Find Him. Deuteronomy 4:29. *"But if... you seek the Lord your God, you will find him, if you look for Him with all your heart and all your soul."* Are you seeking God? And can't seem to find Him? Then check how diligently you are seeking. Is it truly with all your heart and soul? Suppose you lose your wallet in the mall? Or your child strays off in the supermarket? How diligently would you seek? Do you believe that your wallet exists and can be found? Do you believe that your child exists and can be found? As you seek the Lord, do you believe that He exists and can be found? Hebrews 11:6 *"...anyone who comes to God must believe that He exists and that He rewards those who diligently seek Him."*

Out Of Death And Into Life. Deuteronomy 6:13 *"... He brought us out... to bring us in and give us the land He promised under oath to our forefathers."* Here it is again. "He brought us out... to bring us in." Have you allowed God to bring you out of sin and into righteousness, out of guilt and into freedom, out of darkness and into light, out of despair and into hope? Have you arrived yet in your own personal "Promised Land" - the Promised Land where Jesus is, where there is abundant life, filled with love, joy, hope, peace, patience, kindness, forgiveness, goodness, faithfulness, gentleness and self-control? In John 10:27-28 Jesus said: *"My sheep hear my voice, and I know them, and they follow me. And I give unto them eternal life; and they shall never perish..."* Have you followed Jesus out of eternal death and into eternal life?

Jesus In The Old Testament. Deuteronomy 6 and 8. In the Luke 4 description of Jesus' temptation by Satan in the desert, Jesus quotes Moses three times in answering Satan. First, Jesus answers Satan quoting from Deut. 8:3, *"...man does not live by bread alone".* Second, Jesus answers Satan quoting from Deut. 6:13, *"It is written: 'Worship the Lord your God, serve Him only...'".* Third, Jesus answers Satan quoting Deut. 6:16. *"It is written: 'Do not put the Lord your God to the test.'"* Never let anyone tell you that the Old Testament is not really relevant to being a Christian. Jesus confirmed the importance of the Old Testament by quoting it often. Jesus also told the Jewish leaders: *"These are the Scriptures* (the Old

Testament - that's all they had) *that testify about me...* " (John 5:19). Both the Old Testament <u>and</u> the New Testament testify about Jesus.

Absorb The Word. Deuteronomy 11:18-21. *"Fix these words of mine in your hearts and minds, tie them as symbols on your hands and bind them on your foreheads. Teach them to your children, talking about them when you sit at home and when you walk along the road, when you lie down and when you get up. Write them on the door frames of your houses and on your gates so that your days and the days of your children may be many..."* Do you want your days to be "many" (prosperous, fruitful, joyful, hopeful, pleasing to God)? Then saturate your mind and heart in the Word of God. Do you want your children's days to be prosperous, fruitful, joyous, hopeful, pleasing to God? Then saturate their minds and hearts in the Word of God.

Rejoice In Him. Deuteronomy 12:18b. *"... you are to rejoice before the Lord in everything you put your hand to."* As a Christian, the whole of your life - your family life, your professional life, your recreational life - is to be one of rejoicing before the Lord. Why can we do this? Because as the hymn, "Great is Thy Faithfulness," states, He gives us "strength for today, and bright hope for tomorrow." What more do we need?

Now Choose Life. Deuteronomy 30:19-20. *"This day... I have set before you life and death, blessings and curses. Now choose life so that you and your children may live, and that you may love the Lord your God, listen to His voice, and hold fast to Him. For the Lord is your life..."* Choices. Life is made up of choices. Right choices. Wrong choices. God does not force us. He "sets before us" the options, lays out the consequences, advises us, and then lets us make the decisions. Of course, we can't choose our past. It is fixed. We can't choose our parents, our skin color, our athletic ability, our IQ, our nationality, or where we were born, or what we have done in the past. But we CAN choose our future. What will you choose for your future? Will you choose life and blessings? -- or death and curses. It is your choice. It is no one else's choice. You may be able to blame your past on someone or something besides yourself. But not your future. It is your choice - and yours only. God advises: *"Now choose life..."* And don't forget: *"The Lord is your life."*

Joshua

Joshua. The first five books of the Bible were written by Moses. The sixth book was written by Joshua, who was executive officer to Moses for 40 years.

The Word in Your Life. Joshua 1:8-9. *"...meditate on (God's Word) day and night. Be careful to do everything written in it. Then you will be prosperous and successful. Have I not commanded you, 'Be strong and courageous?' Do not be terrified. Do not be discouraged, for the Lord your God will be with you wherever you go."* These two verses contain three of the major themes found throughout all Scripture:

1. Fill your heart and mind with the Word of God. Make it the central theme of your life. Love it. Believe it. Practice what it says, and your life will have meaning and purpose and significance. David says the same thing in the first of his psalms. *"Blessed... is the man whose delight is in the Law of the Lord, who meditates in it day and night. He shall be like a tree planted by the rivers of water, which yields fruit, whose leaves do not wither, and he prospers..."*

2. Living a life pleasing to God is not easy. There are many obstacles. And there are enemies out there. It is not for the lazy or faint of heart. God knows this. So He commands us to be strong and courageous, to choose confidence over fear, hope over despair. Centuries later, Paul repeats this theme. *"... Acquit yourselves like men. Be strong." (1 Corinthians 16:13).*

3. We are not alone. In this difficult and arduous but joyful and hopeful task of living the Christian life, God is with us wherever we go, to give us strength, comfort and hope.

Repent - the Necessary Act Of A Guilty Heart. Joshua 7:10-12 *"The Lord said to Joshua, 'Stand up! What are you doing down on your face? Israel has sinned. They have violated my covenant which I have commanded them to keep... I will not be with you anymore unless you destroy whatever among you is evil and needs to be destroyed."* Joshua, the leader of Israel appointed by God, was praying. He was acknowledging to God the sins of Israel. But God stopped him from praying and told him to get up and stamp out the sinful practices of the Israelites. And if Joshua doesn't, God will no longer be with him or with the Israelites. Prayer is not enough. Confession is not enough. God demands repentance. Sin cuts us off from God. *"Your sins have separated you from God"* (Isaiah 59:2). God's presence with us is conditional. He withdraws His presence if we knowingly persist in sin. We must confess - and repent, i.e., stamp that sin out of our lives.

Speak The Truth. Do The Truth. Joshua 14:7-8 *"... and I (Caleb) brought back a report according to my convictions, but my brothers, who went with me, made the hearts of the people melt with fear."* Caleb was a man of integrity. He told it like he saw it. He didn't waffle or sugar coat the facts. He could not be stampeded by the majority. The vote was 8 to 2 against Caleb. He reported *"according to my convictions."* Many years ago, in the exercise room of the West Point gym, there was a placard which stated, "Stand up for what you stand for." God is not looking for wimps. God wants men and women who have iron wills, who will speak and do the truth regardless of the consequences.

Never Quit. Joshua 14:10-11. *"... Here I (Caleb) am today, eighty-five years old. I am still as strong today as the day Moses sent me out. I'm just as vigorous to go out to battle now as I was then (over 40 years ago)."* God has not set a retirement age. We are to continue in His service until the day He calls us Home. We are to keep ourselves both physically and mentally vigorous - looking for opportunities to go out to do battle for Him again.

Speak the Truth. Do the Truth. Again and Again. Joshua 23:14. *"Now I am about to go the way of all the earth. You know with all your heart and soul that not one of all the good promises the Lord your God gave you has failed. Every promise has been fulfilled; not one has failed."* God keeps his promises. Authentic faith calls us to believe God and live by His promises. The Scripture is full of God's promises. There is an old hymn titled, "Standing on the Promises." That is the Christian way. Stand on His promises. The apostle Peter states, *"... God has given us his very great and precious promises so that through them (standing on them) you may achieve God's divine nature and escape the corruption which is in the world, caused by evil desires."* (2 Peter 4)

Ending Well. Joshua 24:14-15. *"Now fear the Lord and serve Him with all faithfulness. Throw away (all other gods). But if serving the Lord seems undesirable to you, then choose for yourselves this day whom you will serve... But as for me and my household, we will serve the Lord."* Joshua was 110 years old when he threw out this gauntlet before the children of Israel for the final time before his death. Joshua ended well - still standing on the promises, still leading the nation of Israel, still leading his family, still serving the Lord. Will you also end well and thus gain the eternal reward? Or will you bloom brightly for a season and then revert to a life of indifference, sin and disobedience, reaping the 'reward' of death and destruction. This is also one of God's promises.

Judges

Teaching The Next Generation. Judges 2:7 and 10. *"The people served the Lord throughout the lifetime of Joshua and the elders who outlived him... After that whole generation had died, another generation grew up who knew neither the Lord nor what He had done for Israel. Then the Israelites did evil in the eyes of the Lord..."* Freedom, justice, truth, respect for human life - all of the wisdom and values we hold dear as a society, and upon which our nation was founded, - even our blessed Christian faith - will die out in just one generation unless we teach these values, and the faith from which these values were derived, to our children and all of the members of the next generation.

Stand Up For What You Stand For. Judges 6:27. *"So Gideon took ten of his servants and did as the Lord told him. But because he was afraid of his family and the men of the town, he did it at night rather than in the daytime."* Whom do we fear most - man or God? Whom do we serve - man or God? Who holds the promise of eternal life in His hands - man or God? Who is our ultimate judge - man or God? Why do we slink around in the darkness, fearful that someone will find out that we are Christians, hiding the light of the knowledge of Jesus Christ 'under a bushel?' A young college graduate, a Christian, was hired as a junior executive in a large corporation. That weekend the corporation hosted a stag party at a hunting lodge for all the recently hired junior executives. The young man confided to his wife that he was fearful about going because as a Christian he might not be 'accepted.' At the end of the weekend, his wife asked him how it went. He replied that everything went fine. "No one found out that I was a Christian."

God's Design For Society. Judges 21:25. *"In those days Israel had no king; everyone did as he saw fit."* Without civil government, societal anarchy prevails. God established three great human institutions, designed to provide an orderly society in which people may live and prosper in freedom, peace and security. All of these institutions are authoritative. The first institution established was the family. The husband was to be the authority in the family. The second was the church. The priests were to be the authorities in the church. And the third was civil government. The king was to be the authority in civil government. However, all of these institutions are flawed through sin. So there must be checks and balances. But this does not invalidate the basic fact that all three great institutions - the family, the church and the government - must retain their authoritative nature. Otherwise, there is family anarchy, church anarchy and societal anarchy.

Ruth

Making The Right Choice. Ruth 1:16. *"But Ruth replied* (to Naomi, her widowed mother in law) *'Don't urge me to leave you or turn back from you. Where you go, I will go, and where you stay I will stay. Your people will be my people and your God my God. Where you die I will die, and there I will be buried.'"* Ruth, in her twenties, childless and recently widowed, had a choice to make. Either return to her homeland and look for another husband, or stay with her mother-in-law and be her lifelong companion. Ruth chose the latter - service above self. This is always the right choice.

Service As A Sacrifice To God. Ruth 2:2, 7. *"And Ruth...said to Naomi, 'Let me go to the fields and pick up the leftover grain...' Naomi said to her, 'Go ahead my daughter.' ... She went into the field and worked steadily* (in the sun) *from morning until* (late afternoon) *except for a short rest in the shelter."* Service is hard work. It is not accompanied by background music or commercial breaks or crowd applause. The only reward for service is the sure knowledge that it is the right thing to do.

Godly Leadership. Ruth 2:4-5. *"Boaz* (who owned the field) *arrived from Bethlehem and greeted the harvesters saying, 'The Lord be with you'. 'The Lord bless you', they called back. Boaz asked the foreman of the harvesters, 'Whose young woman is that?' The foreman replied, 'She is the Moabitess who came back from Moab with Naomi.'"* Here is a great example of leadership. Boaz has employed capable workers and has appointed a reliable foreman to supervise the work. Boaz comes to check on the work. He greets the workers cordially, with godly respect. He recognizes their hard and effective work. He trusts them. They respond to him with a blessing from God. They respect Boaz. They are happy to see him come. They are eager to show him what they have accomplished. Boaz, the competent, confident, caring leader, has established a bond of loyalty and respect with his workers and their foreman. Boaz then notices Ruth gleaning in the field. He inquires about her - respectfully - calling her a "young woman". There is no crudeness or harshness about Boaz. He is an "officer and a gentleman."

Noble Character. Ruth 2:8-12, 3:11. *"So Boaz said to Ruth, 'My daughter, listen to me. Don't go and glean in another field and don't go away from here. Stay here ...' At this Ruth bowed down with her face to the ground and asked, 'Why have I found such favor in your eyes that you notice me - a foreigner.' Boaz replied, 'I have been told all about what you have done for your mother-in-law since the death of your husband... May the Lord repay you for what you have done. May you* *be richly rewarded by the Lord, the God of Israel, under whose wings you have come to take refuge... All my fellow townsmen know that you are a woman of <u>noble character</u>.'"* Ruth's unselfish service had earned her the highest accolade and best reputation any young woman could ever hope to achieve - to be known as a woman of "noble character."

God Honors Right Choices. Ruth 4:13. *"So Boaz took Ruth and she became his wife."* The marriage took place after an honorable and open courtship. *"And the Lord enabled her to conceive, and she gave birth to a son."* (who became the grandfather of David, the King.) Ruth did it right. She chose service over husband hunting. And eventually God rewarded her with a godly husband. In 1 Corinthians 7, the Apostle Paul addresses the situation of young, unmarried women. Paraphrased and summarized, Paul says don't make husband hunting the focus of your life. Instead, make the Lord's service the focus of your life. Find a ministry, a work which honors the Lord, which you can perform for your entire life, and devote yourself enthusiastically to that ministry. Give yourself fully to the cause of Christ, as a giving person, not a getting person. You will become known as a woman of 'noble character.' And then, in His own time and if He pleases, the Lord will give you a godly husband.

1 Samuel

Evil Religious Leaders. 1 Samuel 1:3, 2:12, 2:17, 2:22, 3:13, 4:10 *"...Hophni and Phienas, the two sons of Eli, were priests of the Lord...they were evil men. They had no regard for the Lord...The sin of the sons of Eli was very great...They forced the women who served at the Tent of Meeting to have sex with them... His sons made themselves contemptible... the Philistines fought the Israelites ...the slaughter was very great ...The Ark of God was captured ... Eli's sons died."* It is a tragic fact of life that some religious leaders are frauds, impostors, evil men. Such were Eli's sons. Because of their high and exalted positions, we tend to trust and believe people in authority in the church and religious organizations. But like all institutions run by humans, churches and religious organizations are infected with sin. Jesus warned us not to follow *"all who say, 'Lord, Lord'...but who do not obey (my commandments)."* He spoke of the Pharisees as, "Shining on the outside. Corrupt on the inside." Be careful whom you follow. Is he or she living in obedience to the Word of God? That is the test!

Successful As A Priest. Failure As A Father. 1 Samuel 2:22, 3:13. *"Now Eli... heard about everything his sons were doing... and he failed to restrain them."* Eli carried out his priestly duties faithfully for many, many years. But he allowed his sons, who were subordinate to him, not only because they were sons but also because they were priests, to run wild. *God said to Eli, "Why do you honor your sons more than me"* (2:29). In God's eyes, Eli was honoring his sons more than he was honoring the Lord because he was allowing his sons to desecrate the priesthood. And as a result, God judged the house of Eli and took the priesthood out of his hands and gave it to Samuel. Our charge as fathers is to raise up our sons *"in the nurture and admonition of the Lord,"* teaching them to follow the Lord in obedience to His way of life. Will it be said of us: "He was a success as a military professional, but he was a failure as a father?"

Telling The Truth To Power. 1 Samuel 3:15. *"Samuel lay down until morning...He was afraid to tell Eli the vision...then Eli asked Samuel (who was probably about 10 years old), 'What was it God said to you last night... do not keep it from me?' So Samuel told Eli everything, hiding nothing from him. Then Eli said, 'He is the Lord. Let Him do what is good in His eyes.'"* In a night vision, God had told Samuel that God was about to withdraw the priesthood from the house of Eli. Why? Because Eli knew about the wicked conduct of his sons who were also priests, but had failed to do anything about it. Samuel, still a child serving in the House of the Lord under the tutelage of Eli, was afraid to tell Eli the bad news. But

Eli, ruler and judge of Israel, wanted to know the truth. So Samuel gave it to him - the whole nine yards. Eli, godly man that he was, accepted the truth.

Lessons:

+ Leaders are granted the requisite authority to carry out their responsibilities. If they fail to use that authority to carry out their responsibilities, they should be replaced by someone who will.

+ Subordinates must be bold to tell their superiors the truth, even though it may not be pleasant. Bad news does not improve with age.

+ It is not enough simply to know the truth. Leaders must have the moral courage to do what truth requires.

+ Good leaders will welcome the truth and, if necessary, force it out of their subordinates.

+ A good rule: "Tell your boss what he needs to know, not what he wants to hear."

Failure To Learn. 1 Samuel 8:1, 3. *"When Samuel grew old, he appointed his sons as judges of Israel... but his sons did not walk in his (Samuel's) ways. They turned aside after dishonest gain and accepted bribes, and perverted justice."* Incredibly, Samuel failed to learn from the poor example of his predecessor, Eli. Like Eli, Samuel was a success as a priest but a failure as a father. He failed to train up his children in the way they should go. As a result, God took power out of the hands of Samuel and his sons and gave it to Saul, who became the first king of Israel.

Righteous Anger. 1 Samuel 11:6. *"When Saul heard the words of the messengers, the Spirit of God came upon him in power, and he burned with anger."* Saul was the new king, anointed by God. The messengers brought word that the heathen Ammonites were about to torture the citizens of a distant Israelite city. When Saul heard this, *"The Spirit of God came upon him in power, and he burned with anger."* Saul immediately organized an attack against the Ammonites and defeated them soundly, thus preventing the atrocity. Are you in such a close relationship with God that when you hear of an injustice, His Spirit causes you to burn with anger and seek ways to correct the injustice? Or are you complacent and think it isn't your problem, so why get involved? Are you complacent about drug abuse, alcohol abuse, sexual abuse, child abuse, abuse of authority, abortion, euthanasia, corruption, injustice, discrimination (racial, religious, ethnic, gender), cheating, gossip, dishonesty, slander? Perhaps the Spirit of God has not yet come upon you in power, because when He does, these horrible social evils will make you burn with anger and you will want to get involved and do something to correct them. Romans 12:9 commands us to *"hate what is evil."* Intolerant? Yes! A Christian should be intolerant of evil.

Beautiful Takeoff But Crashed In Flames. 1 Samuel 28:7-10. *"... The Lord has turned away from you (King Saul) and become your enemy... The Lord has taken the kingdom out of your hands and given it to...David... because you did not obey the Lord..."* King Saul started off strong. He trusted God and obeyed him. But as the years went by, he began to lean on his own understanding. God would tell him what to do and King Saul would obey most of what he had been told, but would either add a little or subtract a little, feeling that he knew better than God what was really the best thing to do. At first he "inquired of God" before he made a decision. Later he went ahead and decided without praying first. Saul offered sacrifices. God wanted obedience. As Saul turned away from God, his kingship became more and more destitute spiritually. Final result: God abandoned him and turned the kingdom over to David. Over the last 60 years, we have seen hundreds of young people begin strong in their Christian pilgrimage but eventually crash in flames. The reason? They stopped believing and obeying what God has stated in His Word. Will you end strong?

2 Samuel

How Will You Be Remembered? 2 Samuel 8:15. *"David reigned over all Israel, doing what was just and right for all his people".* - 2 Samuel 23:3-4. *"The God of Israel spoke, the Rock of Israel said to me: 'When one rules over men in righteousness, when he rules in the fear of God, he is like the light in the morning at sunrise on a cloudless morning, like the brightness after rain that brings the grass from the earth.'"* Are you in a position of authority - military leader, pastor, youth leader, business executive, school teacher, father, mother? Will you be remembered as one who is like the light of morning, like the sunshine after rain who brings forth the best in your people? Will your troops say, "The finest days of my whole military service were when I was in the (your unit), commanded by (your name)?" Will your children say, "My father was a righteous man who feared God. He was like sunshine to us. We reveled in his justice and his love. He brought out the best in us." If this is the way you want to be remembered, then do what is just and right for all of your people, as David did.

A Sordid Tale, A Terrible Truth. 2 Samuel 1-2, 10-12, 14-15. *"In the course of time, Amnon ... became infatuated with Tamar, his beautiful half sister. Amnon was frustrated to the point of illness because Tamar was a virgin and it seemed impossible for him to do anything to her... (but) Amnon (pretending to be very sick), said to Tamar, 'Bring my food into my bedroom so that I can eat it out of your hand.' And Tamar brought the bread she had prepared for him into his bedroom. But when she started to feed it to him, he grabbed her and said, 'Come to bed with me, my sister'. 'Don't, my brother' she said to him, 'Don't force me...don't do this wicked thing'... But he refused to listen to her, and since he was stronger than she, he raped her. Then Amnon hated her with intense hatred and he said, 'Get up and get out.'"* Herein lies a terrible truth every girl should understand and remember. After a man successfully entices a young virgin to have sex with him, he immediately loses respect for her, despises her, and throws her out of his life. He has made his 'kill' and now wants nothing more to do with his miserable victim. Why would God have included this in his Word except as a warning to innocent young girls.

A Great Example Of Personal Integrity. 2 Samuel 24:18-24. *"On that day, Gad (the prophet) went to David and said to him, 'Go up and build an altar to the Lord on the threshing floor of Araunah the Jebusite.' So David went up as the Lord had commanded him through Gad. When Araunah looked and saw the king and his men coming, he went out and bowed down before the king with his face on the* *ground. Araunah said, 'Why has my lord the king come to his servant?' David replied: 'To buy the threshing floor so I can build an altar to the Lord that the plague on my people might be stopped.' Araunah said to David, 'Let my lord the king take whatever he pleases and offer it up. Here are oxen for the burnt offering...O king, Araunah gives this all to the king...' But David replied, 'No, I insist on paying you for it. I will not sacrifice to the Lord my God burnt offerings that cost me nothing.' So David bought the threshing floor and the oxen...offered the sacrifice... and the plague on Israel was stopped."* As King, David would not take advantage of a private citizen and let that private citizen pay for something that David should pay for. This is personal integrity.

1 Kings

Ruling with Wisdom. 1 Kings 3:5-10. *"At Gibeon the Lord appeared to Solomon in a dream, and God said, 'Ask for whatever you want me to give you.' Solomon answered, ... 'give your servant a discerning heart to govern your people and to distinguish between right and wrong' ... The Lord was pleased that Solomon had asked for this. So God said to him, 'Since you have asked for this and not for long life or wealth for yourself, nor have you asked for the death of your enemies but for discernment in administering justice, I will do what you have asked. I will give you a wise and discerning heart.'"* Is God interested in how people are governed? The answer is yes. In every area of life - political, military, business, church, family - the answer is yes. God wants His people governed by leaders who have wise and discerning hearts, who know right from wrong, and who will walk in His ways and obey His commands.

Get Things In The Right Order. 1 Kings 5:3-6. *"(Solomon said to Hiram) ... 'You know that because of the wars waged against my father David from all sides he could not build a temple for the Lord his God until the Lord put his enemies under his feet. But now the Lord my God has given me peace on every side and there is no adversary or disaster. I intend therefore to build a temple for the Lord my God as the Lord told my father David, when he said, 'Your son whom I will put on the throne in your place will build the temple for my Name.'"* David wanted to build a temple for God but God told him no. It was David's job to establish security and peace for His people. His son and successor, Solomon, would build the temple. This was God's order of things: establish security, then build the temple. Often, with the best of intentions, we get things in the wrong order. A young man was in a prestigious Christian college. He was very 'people oriented'. He spent almost every night until the wee hours walking around the halls and talking with other students who had personal problems. Result? He flunked out. He should have spent more time studying. He got things in the wrong order. College is preparation for ministry - like establishing security and peace for the nation before building the temple. Eager young Christians just finishing high school sometimes want to get right into full time ministry. "I want to be a missionary - NOW." But preparation is necessary first. Go to college, and then maybe seminary, and then 'build the temple'. Jesus was 30 years old before he began his active ministry. The earlier years were spent in preparation.

The End Game. 1 Kings, chapters 11-22. *"Nadad did evil in the eyes of the Lord ... Asa did what was right in the eyes of the Lord... Basha did evil ... Jehoshaphat* *did what was right... Judah did evil ... Asa did what was right ...Omri did evil in the sight of the Lord..."* The list goes on and on in these chapters. This is how God described the kings of Israel and Judah. "He did right ... He did evil." One liners. The end game. The big question -- for each one of us -- "Am I doing what is right in the eyes of the Lord? At the end of the day, will people say "He did evil," or "He did what is right," If I were called into His presence today, would He say, 'Well done, thou good and faithful servant?'"

2 Kings

How Refreshing! 2 Kings 12:14-15. *"(The money) was paid to the workmen, who used it to repair the temple. They did not require an accounting from those to whom they gave the money to pay the workers because they acted in complete honesty."* How refreshing to hear a report that someone acted in complete honesty. How different from our world in which corruption is the primary sin of the times. The Bible teaches that the love of money is the root of all evil. In this case, the people who handled money acted in complete honesty. No accounting. No receipts or notarized signatures. No guarantees. No sworn statements. No triple paged, legally sufficient contracts. Just plain honesty. Trustworthiness. How refreshing. Can people trust me to "act in complete honesty."

Cause And Effect. 2 Kings 17:15. *"... They followed worthless idols and themselves became worthless"* (NIV). There is a biblical principle here. We become like what or whom we follow. If we follow falsehood we will become false ourselves. If we follow materialism we will become materialistic. If we follow pornography or highly sensual movies, we will become sexually perverted. On the other hand, if we follow the example of Jesus Christ we will become like Jesus Christ. To the early disciples, Jesus said, "Follow me", and they became men and women of sublime godliness, of towering courage, of ageless influence for good - like Jesus Christ. Am I following the worthless idols of wealth, power, pleasure, self-indulgence? Or am I following the matchless example of Jesus Christ?

Worshiping God And Mammon. 2 Kings 17:33. *"They worshiped the Lord, but they also served their own gods in accordance with the customs (of the society)..."* This is an accurate commentary on the religiosity of our times. We go to church on Sunday and participate with great enthusiasm in the worship music and the companionship of our friends. We proclaim in song, within the confines of our church, our profound and eternal love for God and His ways. And then we go out into the crowd and become one of them. We go to the mall and revel in the luxury of materialism. We catch the latest PG rated movie (or R rated if no one sees us) and get enough sexual excitement to titillate our imaginations for the next few days. We get up late, miss our promised time with the Lord, complain about breakfast, and leave for school or work without a kind word to any family member. We yell at the driver who cuts in front of us and then do the same to the slowpoke ahead of us. A keen observer of the present day practice of Christianity made this statement. "Seventy years ago Christians lived disciplined, sacrificial, unselfish, devoted, frugal, moral lives, and seldom talked to anyone about their faith. Today Christians live undisciplined, self-indulgent, grasping, superficial, wasteful, immoral lives and talk constantly about their faith." Am I trying to play it both ways? Worship God AND mammon? The Bible teaches us that *"... a double minded man is unstable in all his ways."* (James 1:8)

The Power Of The Word. 2 Kings 23:1-3. *"Then the king (Josiah) called together all the elders of Judah and Jerusalem. He went up to the temple of the Lord with the men of Judah, the people of Jerusalem, the priests and the prophets -- all the people from the least to the greatest. He read in their hearing the words of the Book of the Covenant, which had been found in the temple of the Lord. The king stood by the pillar and renewed the covenant in the presence of the Lord... Then all the people pledged themselves to the Covenant."* There was no preaching, no trumpets, no clashing symbols, no praise team, no burnt offerings, no incense. Just the pure, simple reading of the Book of the Covenant; and the king, the elders, the prophets, the priests, and all the people from the least to the greatest pledged themselves to the Covenant. There is power in the Word. *"For the word of God is alive and powerful..."* (Hebrews 4:12). *"Faith comes by hearing the word of God"* (Romans 10:17).

1 Chronicles

Understanding the Times. 1 Chronicles 16:43. *"...men of Issachar, who understood the times and knew what Israel should do--200 chiefs."* This section of 1 Chronicles lists the soldiers by tribe who defected from Saul and joined David. The total exceeded 300,000. Of these, 200 were from the tribe of Issachar. They understood the times and knew what Israel should do.

Here is a nugget for those who aspire to public leadership. Study ancient history. Study modern history. Study sociology. Study psychology. Study international relations. Study government, economics, law and politics. And above all, study the Word of God in its totality. All to the end that you might understand the times and know what our nation should do. Future leaders - do you have a grasp of what the United States of America, as the most wealthy and powerful nation in the world, should be doing now and in the decades to come?

Returning Home to Bless Your Family. 1 Chronicles 16:43. *"Then all of the people left, each to his own home, and David returned home to bless his family."* It had been a massive, joyful celebration. David had had the ark of the Lord returned to Jerusalem. There had been wild dancing in the streets and King David wrote a special psalm for the occasion (1 Chronicles 16:7-36). David was at the high point of his whole reign. He had consolidated the kingdoms of Israel and Judah; he had established peace, security, and order over the entire land; and now he had brought the ark back to Jerusalem. At the end of this day of ultimate triumph, *"... David returned home to bless his family."* David's lifetime example as a husband and father is deeply flawed. But in this case, he did the right thing, and every father should emulate David's example every day. It should be the joyful and thankful practice of every father, at the end of the work day, whether it has been a good day or a bad day, to go home and bless his family.

Taking Responsibility for Your Actions. 1 Chronicles 21:16-17. *"... Then David and the Elders, clothed in sackcloth, fell face downward. David said to God, 'Was it not I who ordered (this disobedience)? I am the one who has sinned and done wrong. These people are but sheep. They have only followed my orders. O Lord my God, let your hand fall upon me and my family but do not let this plague remain on your people.'"* One of the essential qualities of effective leadership is the willingness to stand up and take responsibility for your actions.

The Right Attitude Toward Personal Resources. 1 Chronicles 29:15. *"O Lord* *our God, as for all this abundance that we have provided for building you a temple for your Holy Name, it came from your hand, and all of it belongs to you."* As his final official project before his death, King David draws up the plans for the temple his son Solomon will build, and then raises the money to build it. As an example for the people, David provides millions of dollars from his personal treasure. The people then give generously and the money flowed in. The people rejoice and so does David. In his public prayer of thanksgiving (1 Chronicles 29:10-20), David recognizes that the money which they had given for the building of the temple was not really their own money, but had come from God's hand in the first place. As we accumulate wealth during our lives, will we be constantly aware that it actually comes from God's hand and be willing to give it back to him in ways that will that bring Him glory?

2 Chronicles

The Healing Process. 2 Chronicles 7:14. *"If my people who are called by my name will humble themselves and pray and seek my face and turn from their wicked ways, then I will hear from heaven and will forgive their sin and heal their land."* Note the steps in the process.

We are to:
1. Humble ourselves. This means admit that we have sinned.
2. Pray and seek His face. This means confess our sins to God.
3. Turn from our wicked ways. This means repent.

Then God will:
1. Hear our prayer of confession.
2. Forgive our sins.
3. Restore us to our place of fellowship with Him.

We need to follow this process daily. The Prayer Book leads us in confession of sins of thought, word, and deed; sins of commission and omission; sins both conscious and unconscious. Our part is to admit, confess and repent. God's part is to hear, forgive and restore.

From Power To Pride To Downfall. 2 Chronicles 12:1, 5. *"After Rehoboam's position as king was established and he had become strong, he ... abandoned the Law of the Lord ... and the Lord said, 'Because you have abandoned me I will abandon you to your enemies.'"* 2 Chronicles 26:16. *"But after Huzzah became powerful, his pride led to his downfall. He was unfaithful to the Lord His God..."* It is a law of life that there are no permanent successes. As we climb the ladder toward success, we proclaim loudly that God is our strength. But then when we have reached the top, we abandon God, pound our chests and shout, "See what I have done." And then God walks away from the ladder, it collapses and we are destroyed. We must never forget that everything we have and everything we accomplish comes from God. Many of the great civilizations of history have fallen into this trap of power, pride and downfall.

Justice Comes By The Fear Of The Lord. 2 Chronicles 20:4-7. *"Jehoshaphat... appointed judges in the land... He told them, 'Consider carefully what you do, because you are not judging for man but for the Lord, who is with you whenever you give a verdict. Now let the fear of the Lord rest upon you. Judge carefully, for* *with the Lord our God there is no injustice or partiality or bribery.'"* The Scripture teaches us that, *"the fear of the Lord is the beginning of wisdom."* There is no true wisdom or justice unless it is based on an absolute certainty (a fear) that we are accountable to God for whatever we do. And whatever we do, it must be consistent with His character (justice, mercy, faithfulness). Are we prepared to stand tonight before the God of all Creation and give Him a full account of all of our thoughts, words and deeds?

A Tale Of Two Kings. 2 Chronicles 21:20. *"Jehoram reigned in Jerusalem eight years. He passed away, to no one's regret."* 2 Chronicles 32:33. *"Hezekiah rested with his fathers and was buried on the hill where the tombs of David's descendants are. All Judah and the people of Jerusalem honored him when he died."* Two different leaders. Two ways of life. Two approaches to the use of power and influence. Serving self leads to departure *"to no one's regret."* The way of departure *"with honor"* stems from selfless service on behalf of others. The mark of a godly person, regardless of rank or stature, is that he or she is a giving person, not a getting person.

Good Advice - Bad Advice. 2 Chronicles 10:6,8. *"Then King Rehoboam consulted the elders who had served his father Solomon... But Rehoboam rejected the advice the elders gave him and consulted (and accepted the advice of) the young men who had grown up with him...* "The elders gave good advice. The young men gave bad advice. And the new king suffered the consequences. Do not reject the advice of your elders. They have lived long lives and had much experience. They are much more likely to give good advice than are the young and inexperienced. For the best advice, consult the Bible. Psalm 119:24 states: *"Your statutes are my delight. They are my advisors."*

An Amazing State Of Affairs. 2 Chronicles 16:9. *"For the eyes of the Lord range throughout the earth to strengthen those whose hearts are fully committed to Him."* Picture this in your mind. God is looking out over the whole earth. He looks north, south, east and west -- into every home, school room, university classroom, military unit, business, church -- looking for those whose hearts are fully committed to Him. Why? Because He wants to strengthen them -- for life, for ministry, for great purposes, in hardships, in disappointments, in grief, in sickness, in discouragement -- so that they might persevere and end well. Will you be one of those He finds and strengthens because your heart is fully committed to Him?

Trouble With Your Boss? - Pray for Him. 2 Chronicles 36:22. *"In the first year of Cyrus the King of (the vast empire of) Persia... the Lord moved the heart of*

Cyrus, King of Persia, to make a proclamation throughout his realm (which was very favorable to the Israelites)..." God is fully able to work in the hearts of non-believing presidents, dictators, commanders, teachers, parents and whoever might be directly over you in authority. In 1 Tim. 2:1-2, the Apostle Paul states: *"I urge... that... prayers be made for... kings and all those in authority that we might live peaceable and quiet lives in all godliness and holiness."* We must pray for them. Why? So that we might live peaceable and quiet lives in all godliness and holiness. Having a problem with your superior (parent, teacher, supervisor, military commander) which is preventing you from living a peaceable and quiet life in all godliness and holiness? Try praying for him. And God may move in his heart to act more favorably toward you.

Ezra

In Spite Of His Circumstances. Ezra 7:1, 6, 10. *"...during the reign of Artaxerxes king of Persia, Ezra...came up from Babylon (to Israel). He was a teacher well versed in the Laws of Moses which the Lord ...had given. Ezra devoted himself to the study and observance of the Law of the Lord, and to teaching its decrees and laws in Israel."* Ezra grew up in captivity in Babylon. But he did not allow these adverse circumstances to prevent him from preparing for the great mission God had for him. He studied and prepared, and then he was given the opportunity to return to Israel to teach the Law of the Lord to the Jewish people who had remained there. One of the great American commanders during WW II stated that, in his early years of service before the war, when promotions were slow and pay was low, he studied and prepared himself in the event that someday his nation might call on him for great deeds in battle. What are you doing in these early years of your Christian life? Are you disciplining yourself by the Word of God and preparing for great deeds He may call on you to perform for Him someday in the future?

The Great Opportunity Comes. Ezra 7:6, 11-13, 15, 25. *"... The king had granted to him (Ezra) everything he asked, for the hand of the Lord his God was upon him (Ezra)... Now here is a copy of the letter King Artaxerxes had given to Ezra the priest and teacher, a man learned in matters and decrees of the Lord of Israel. 'Artaxerxes, king of kings, to Ezra, the priest, a teacher of the Lord of the God of Heaven: Greetings. Now I decree that any of the Israelites in my kingdom... who wish to go to Jerusalem with you, may go... you are to take with you the silver and gold that the king and his advisors have freely given to the God of Israel... And you, Ezra, in accordance with the wisdom of your God which you possess, appoint magistrates and judges to administer justice to all the people (in Israel)...'"* In his early years, Ezra had studied and prepared. Like Jesus, he had, *"increased in wisdom and stature, and in favor with God and man."* Like Joseph (a slave in Egypt) and Daniel (a captive in Babylon), Ezra's learning, his discipline, his judgment and his dedication had come to the attention of the king and had impressed him greatly. And now Ezra was appointed by the king to return to Jerusalem to rule the land of the Israelites (still a part of the Persian Empire) in accordance with the Law of the Lord. Are you developing your character and intellect so that when the opportunity comes, you will be prepared to shoulder great responsibility for the Lord?

Ezra's Response. Ezra 7:27. *"Praise be to the Lord, the God of our fathers, who* *has put it into the king's heart to bring honor to the house of the Lord in Jerusalem in this way and who has extended his good favor to me before the king and his advisors and all the king's powerful officials. Because the hand of the Lord was upon me, I took courage and gathered leading men from among the Israelites to go up (to Jerusalem) with me.* " Ezra's first response to the king's decree was to offer praise and thanksgiving to God. What is my first response when God provides something good in my life? When I first get up in the morning, do I praise Him for life, for health, for another day? When I receive a letter or e-mail from a friend, is my first response to praise God? When I receive a good grade on a test, or get a favorable assignment, or am selected for promotion - do I stop and first praise and thank God? When I return from a trip and gather my spouse and children in my arms, are my first words praise and thanksgiving to God for my safe return to my family? Do I recognize that all good things come from Him?

Nehemiah

Nehemiah. The whole book is a nugget. It is the story of a faithful and competent man called by God to perform a difficult task - to rebuild the walls of Jerusalem in the face of strong and sinister opposition, and subsequently to establish a competent and just government in Judah. With great courage, perseverance, discernment and wisdom, Nehemiah eventually succeeds. Let's see why.

The Situation And Nehemiah's Response. Nehemiah 1:3-4. *"(Friends who had just returned from Judah to Persia) said to me, 'Those who survived the exile and are back in the province are in great trouble and disgrace. The wall of Jerusalem is broken down and its gates have been burned with fire.' When I heard these things I sat down and wept. For some days I mourned and fasted and prayed before the God of heaven."* It was during this time of prayer and fasting that Nehemiah received the call of God to go back to Jerusalem and rebuild the wall and the city. Are you deeply distressed by some pending disaster like a family divorce, an ungodly relationship, a moral or ethical failure by a friend or coworker, or your own shipwrecked life which seems to hold no hope or purpose? Fast and pray, and God will give you guidance on what you should do.

Nehemiah Takes Action. Nehemiah 2:4-5, 8. *"The king (Artaxerxes) said to me, 'What is it you want?' Then I prayed to the God of heaven and answered the king. 'If it please the king and if your servant has found favor in your sight, let him send me to the city in Judah where my fathers are buried so that I can rebuild it'... and because the gracious hand of my God was upon me, the king granted my requests."* Nehemiah did not just continue to lay around and mourn. He took action. Nehemiah, through hard work and an excellent spirit, had become a high ranking aide to King Artaxerxes. He took the great personal risk of asking the king (after a quick prayer) for permission to go back to Judah to rebuild the walls of Jerusalem. God had prepared Nehemiah for this moment. The need was great. The call was clear. Nehemiah was prepared. Nehemiah took action. Are you getting ready for what God may call you to do? Are you listening for His call? Do you have the courage to take a great personal risk to follow God's call?

Doing Good Always Brings Opposition. Nehemiah 2:10. *"When Sanballat the Horonite and Tobiah the Ammonite official heard about this (the plan to rebuild the wall) they were very much disturbed that someone had come to promote the welfare of the Israelites."* Nehemiah 4:1. *"When Sanballat heard that we were (actually on site) building the wall, he became angry and was very incensed. He* *ridiculed the Jews ... in the presence of his associates and the army of Samaria..."* Be assured that whenever you begin doing something good, there will be those with evil intentions who will oppose you. It is a fact of life that good will always be opposed by evil. The Apostle Paul speaks of this as 'spiritual warfare.' The forces of good in this world are always at war with the forces of evil. And whenever 'good' becomes weak or complacent, 'evil' will move in and take over. *"Everyone who wants to live a godly life in Christ Jesus will be persecuted (opposed.)"* (2 Timothy 3:12). So don't be surprised when your efforts to be good and do good are strongly opposed by those who do evil. It happens every time.

Lessons In Countering Evil Opposition. *"I went to Jerusalem..."* (Nehemiah 2:11). Keep on going. Nehemiah had just heard of the opposition of Sanballat and Tobiah to his coming to Jerusalem, but he went anyway. -- *"Then I said to them... Come, let us rebuild the wall of Jerusalem..."* (Nehemiah 2: 17). Start the work. In spite of the imminent threat, Nehemiah got things moving. *"We prayed to our God and posted a guard night and day to meet this threat."* (Nehemiah 4:9). Pray for God's help and make provision to defend yourself against your opposition. -- *"After I looked things over, I stood up and said to all the nobles, officials, and the rest of the people, 'Don't be afraid of them. Remember the Lord who is great and awesome'..."* (Nehemiah 4:14). Encourage each other to continue to work in the power of God. --*"Those who (labored) did their work with one hand and held a weapon with the other...(I said) 'Whenever you hear the sound of the trumpet, join us here. Our God will fight for us'...So we continued the work with half of the men holding spears, from the first light of dawn until the stars came out."* (Nehemiah 4:17, 20, 21). Keep working. Stay vigilant. Have an action plan. Keep your armor on. Put your trust in God.

Overcoming Evil. Nehemiah 6:15-16. *"So the wall was completed ... in 52 days. When all of our enemies heard about this and all the surrounding nations saw it, our enemies lost their confidence because they realized that this work had been done with the help of God.* Nehemiah persevered and overcame. Many a great battle has been won because one leader refused to give up. The battle of Midway during World War II is a classic. After three days of disastrous American aircraft losses and the sinking of one American aircraft carrier by the Japanese, Admiral Spruance, USN, decided to fight on for one more day, and on that fourth day, the US Navy sank four Japanese aircraft carriers, turning the tide in the Pacific war in favor of the Americans. Long after WW II, Winston Churchill, great wartime Prime Minister of England, was asked to give a speech to a British Middle School. After a lengthy introduction by the headmaster, Churchill rose, stood in front of the class, and said, "Never give up. Never give up. Never give up". Then he sat down.

The speech was over. But who could ever forget that speech? Overcoming evil requires courage, perseverance, and the faith that God will fight with you for what is good. Never give up!

Dealing With Internal Corruption. Nehemiah 5:6-10. *"When I heard (the people's) outcry and their charges, I was very angry. I pondered them in my mind and then confronted the nobles and the officials. I told them, 'You are extracting usury (illegally high interest rates) from your own countrymen...What you are doing is not right. Shouldn't you walk in the fear of the Lord and avoid the reproach of the Gentiles...Let the exacting of usury stop. Give back to them immediately their fields, vineyards, olive groves and houses.'"* Nehemiah was now the new governor of Judah. Under previous governors, who didn't care about the common people, the rich Jewish nobles and officials, acting as money lenders to the common people, had been charging extremely high interest rates on loans and had been seizing property in payment on those loans. When Nehemiah, who had been appointed governor by King Artaxerxes, arrived and heard about this, he became angry; he called the nobles and officials to account, and he stopped the sinful practice. In every society corruption is endemic. *"The love of money is the root of all evil."* Do evil practices make you angry? Are you willing to confront evil and put a stop to it? In your own personal life? In your family? In your school? In your church? At your workplace? If not, you are giving tacit approval to evil and thus are an accomplice to that evil.

Servant Leadership. Nehemiah 5:14-16. *"From the twentieth year of King Artaxerxes when I was appointed to be the governor in the land of Judah until his thirty second year - twelve years - neither I nor my (staff) ate the food allotted to the governor. But the earlier governors - those preceding me - placed a heavy burden on the people exacting huge taxes in the form of money, food and wine. Their assistants also lorded it over the people. But out of reverence for God, I did not act like that. Instead, I devoted myself to the (interests of the common people.)... I never demanded the food previously allotted to the governor because the burdens on the common people of just earning a living were very great."* Here again we see two completely different examples of leadership. In one instance, the governor demands that the people serve him. In the other, the leader is the servant of the people. Nehemiah went to Jerusalem from a plush job in the court of the king and risked his life to *"promote the welfare of the people."* (Nehemiah 2:10). Nehemiah understood the legitimate purpose of government -- to promote the welfare of the people. Nehemiah denied himself, took up his responsibilities, and executed them faithfully. Jesus says, *"If any man would come after me, he must deny himself and take up his cross and follow me."* (Matt 16:24).

Esther

A Tale of Two Queens

Vashti - Dignity and Courage. Esther 1:1-3, 10-12. *"King Xerxes reigned from his royal throne in the citadel of Susa. In the third year of his reign he gave a banquet for all his nobles and officials. The military leaders of Persia and Media, the princes and the nobles of the provinces were present.... On the seventh day (of the banquet), when King Xerxes was in high spirits from wine, he commanded ...that Queen Vashti appear before him wearing her royal crown in order to display her beauty to the people and nobles, for she was lovely to look at... But Queen Vashti refused to come."* -- The king of Persia was drunk. He gave an order that the queen appear before his guests in order to display her beauty, i.e., her sexual attractiveness. Risking her life and her throne, Queen Vashti refused. She would not allow herself to be displayed and gawked at by the drunken nobles and officials from all around the realm. Instead, she courageously refused. She maintained her dignity - at the loss of her queenship. The Bible teaches that wives should obey their husbands. However, there are two exceptions. First, do not obey if your husband commands you to do something which God forbids. Second, do not obey if your husband forbids you to do something which God commands. God forbids a woman to display herself as an object sexual attraction. Women are to dress modestly. Are you, young woman, demeaning yourself, by the way you dress, seeking to be sexually attractive?

Esther - Beauty. Esther chapter 2. *"Let a search be made (throughout the vast kingdom) for beautiful young virgins for the king ... Let the girl who pleases the king be queen instead of Vashti ... Now there was in the citadel of Susa a Jew of the tribe of Benjamin named Mordecai. Mordecai had a cousin named Hadassah whom he had brought up because she had neither father or mother. This girl, who was also known as Esther, was lovely in form and features... During the search for a new queen for King Xerxes, Esther was taken to the king's palace... The king was attracted to Esther more than any of the other young women and she won his favor and approval more than any of the other virgins. So he set a royal crown on her head and made her queen instead of Vashti."* A beauty contest was held throughout the entire kingdom to find a new queen for King Xerxes. Esther was beautiful in form and features. Esther won. She was crowned queen. She was now in a position to do great things for her people, the Jews, who were being persecuted throughout the realm.... Not every girl is *"lovely in form and features."* But if God has graced you with physical beauty, use it to the glory of God -- as Esther did.

Esther - Courage. Esther chapters 2 - 4. *"...Esther had kept secret her family background and nationality just as Mordecai had told her to do, for she continued to follow Mondecai's instructions as she had done when he was bringing her up... King Xerxes gave honor to Haymen, a noble in the king's court ... elevating him and giving him a seat of honor higher than all the other nobles ... Haymen looked for a way to destroy all ... the Jews throughout the whole kingdom of Xerxes ... When Mordecai heard of this... he asked Esther to go into the king's presence... and plead with him for her people... Esther responded to Mordecai that any man or woman who approached the king without being summoned would be put to death, unless the king extended the golden scepter ... Mordecai answered... 'If you remain silent at this time ... you and your father's family will perish. And who knows but that you have come to the royal position for such a time as this'. Esther responded, 'I will go to the king...and if I perish, I perish.'* -- This conversation between Mordecai and Esther has thundered down the centuries as an example of a monumental challenge and a fearless response. When faced with a desperate situation, when we could either speak or be silent, act or remain idle, fight on or withdraw, each of us should ask, "Have I come to this position of authority for such a time as this?" Esther knew the risk to herself if she went to the king without being summoned. She also knew the risk to her people if she did nothing. Esther's response should be our response, "I will take the risk. I will do the right thing. And *'if I perish, I perish.'"* -- Like Vashti before her, Esther was willing to risk her life and her queenship to do the right thing.

Esther - Prudent and Bold. Esther, chapters 5, 7. *"Three days later (as her friends were fasting and praying) Esther put on her royal robes and stood... in front of the king's hall. The king was sitting on his royal throne... facing the entrance. When he saw Queen Esther standing in the court, he was pleased with her and held out the gold scepter... Esther approached and touched the tip of the scepter. The King then asked, 'What is it Queen Esther? What is your request?' 'If it please the king,' replied Esther, 'Let the king, together with Haymen, come to a banquet I have prepared...So the King and Haymen went to the banquet. The king again asked Esther, 'What is your petition?' Esther replied, 'Let the king and Haymen come tomorrow to another banquet. Then I will answer the king's question.' So (the next day) the king and Haymen again went to dine with Queen Esther... the King again asked, 'What is your petition?' Then Queen Esther answered, ' Spare my people. I and my people have been sold for destruction and slaughter and annihilation...' King Xerxes asked Queen Esther, 'Where is the man who would do such a thing?' Esther said, 'The adversary and the enemy is this vile*

Haymen.'...The king stood up in a rage... and said... Hang him on (the gallows).'
So they hanged Haymen." ---- As her friends fasted and prayed, Esther planned carefully and brilliantly. She formulated a plan which would please the king and bring the king and Haymen together at the critical instant. She added suspense by planning two banquets instead of just one. She approached the king in all of her feminine loveliness and queenly dignity, and started the plan in motion. Then, at the second banquet, she boldly sprung the trap for Haymen. The king, enraged, ordered Haymen to be hanged immediately. And the villain, who had plotted the destruction of the Jews throughout the realm, was no more. Regardless of how honorable, righteous and necessary is the objective, plans to achieve that objective must be carefully and prudently developed, and preceded by prayer and fasting.

Esther - Perseverance. Esther, chapters 8 and 9. *"That same day, King Xerxes gave Esther the estate of Haymen, the enemy of the Jews. And Mordecai came into the presence of the king,... The king took off his signet ring, which he had reclaimed from Haymen, and presented it to Mordecai... Esther again pleaded with the king, falling at his feet and weeping. She begged him to put an end to the evil plan which Haymen had devised against the Jews. She asked of the king... 'Let an order be written overruling the dispatches that Haymen... devised and wrote to destroy the Jews in all the king's provinces.' King Xerxes replied to Queen Esther and to Mordecai the Jew, 'Write another decree in the King's name on behalf of the Jews as seems best to you, and seal it with the king's signet ring ...The king's decree granted to the Jews in every province the right to assemble and protect themselves... Mordecai wrote letters to the Jews in 127 provinces of the kingdom of Xerxes -- words of good will and assurance. (Upon receipt of these documents, the Jews throughout the realm) observed days of feasting and joy and giving presents of food to one another and gifts to the poor."* Esther did not stop with the execution of Haymen. She pled the case of the Jews before the King and he then sent an edict out to all the provinces granting the Jews all the rights and privileges of citizenship. These Jews were the descendants of those who had been carried into exile from Jerusalem by King Nebuchadnezzar four generations earlier. Esther persevered until all of the Jews in Persia were made full citizens of the kingdom. She used her authority as queen for the good of her people. Are you thinking about dropping out of college or quitting your job or compromising your integrity or moving away from home -- because the going is tough? Then think of the perseverance of Esther. Keep on keeping on until the task is complete, and our Lord will say to you, *"Well done, thou good and faithful servant."*

Job

Suffering, Perseverance, Faithfulness, Contemplation, Despair, Hope, Revelation, Confession, Obedience, Restoration

Dealing with Tragedy. Job 1:20-21. *"At this, Job got up and tore his robe and shaved his head. Then he fell to the ground in worship and said: 'Naked I came from my mother's womb ...The Lord gave and the Lord has taken away; may the name of the Lord be praised.'"* Job had just learned that all of his livestock had been destroyed and all of his servants and children had been killed. His first act was an act of worship. He recognized that everything he had 'possessed' - livestock, servants and children - had been given him by God and it was God's right to take them back. In total humility and faith, Job was able to say, *"May the Name of the Lord be praised."* We do not achieve significance by what we possess or by what we have achieved, but by our relationship with God.

Ultimate Faith. Job 13:15. *"Though He slay me, yet will I trust Him."* Stripped of possessions, servants and children, and now afflicted with horribly painful sores from head to toe, Job looked death in the face and held on to his faith in and his relationship with God. Centuries later, the prophet Isaiah proclaimed, *"If you do not stand firm in your faith, you will not stand at all."* (Isaiah 7:9b). And even later, the Apostle Peter replied to Jesus, *"Lord to whom shall we go? You have the words of eternal life"* (John 6:68). We praise God that in whatever the circumstance, there is a place to go. And that is the place of complete trust and faith in God and His goodness.

Despair. Job 14:10. Job 17:1, 11, 15-16 *"... man dies and is laid low; he breathes his last and is no more ... My spirit is broken, my days are cut short ... my plans are shattered, and so are the desires of my heart ... where then is my hope? Who can see any hope for me? Will it go down to the gates of death? Will we descend together into the dust?"* Unless a person has sunk into the depths of despair and contemplated the black hole of eternal nothingness and oblivion, he cannot truly understand the magnitude and magnificence of God's gift of eternal life through Jesus Christ our Lord. It is not a mark of weakness or sin to sink into despair. It is the beginning of salvation.

Hope. Job 14:14. Job 19:25-27. *"If a man dies, will he live again? ... I know that my Redeemer lives and in the end He will stand upon the earth. After my skin has been destroyed, yet in my flesh I will see God; myself will see Him with my own* *eyes - I, and not another. How my heart yearns within me."* Having sunk to the depths of despair, and having asked the timeless question, *"If a man dies, will he live again?"* Job makes the ultimate statement of faith, *"I know that my Redeemer lives."* Would that each of us live our lives with that magnificent statement ever in our conscious minds and hearts. *"I know that my Redeemer lives."*

Treasuring the Word. Job 23:12b. *"I have treasured the words of His mouth more than my daily bread."* It can't get any plainer than this. Would you rather read/hear the Word of God than to eat? Of course eating is necessary to sustain physical life. But so also is 'eating' the Word of God necessary to sustain spiritual life. Someone once said, "God's word will keep me from sin, or sin will keep me from God's Word." David said, *"Blessed is the man...whose delight is in the law of the Lord."* (Psalm 1), and again, *"I have hidden your Word in my heart (memorized it) so that I might not sin against you."* (Psalm 119:105)

The Fear of the Lord. Job 28:28. *"And God said to man, 'The Fear of the Lord. That is wisdom.'"* The Bible says a lot about loving God. That is the first commandment -- *"Love the Lord your God with all your heart, soul and mind."* (Matthew 22:37) But the Bible also says a lot about fearing God. I loved my father. He was a very caring and generous man. He also had very high moral standards, and I knew that if I violated those standards and he found out about it, I would be severely punished. This caused me to fear him as well as love him. The Bible says that I am accountable to God for everything I think, say, and do. And I can't hide my sins from God. The absolute certainty that God will do exactly as he has promised strikes fear in my heart and makes me consider very carefully what I should think, speak and do. The psalmist said, *"The fear of the Lord is the beginning of wisdom"* (Psalm 111:10a). Living in recognition that we are accountable to God is both Fear and Wisdom.

Men, Let's Skip This Verse. Job 31:1. *"(Job said), I made a covenant with my eyes not to look lustfully at a girl."* Why did Job make such a radical and difficult covenant? Does it really matter if a man looks lustfully at a girl, so long as he does not go any farther? The Apostle James writes, *"But every man is tempted when he is drawn away by his own lust and enticed. Then when lust has conceived it brings forth sin: and sin, when it is finished, brings forth death."* (James 1:14-15). If a man spends time fantasizing sexually about a girl he will eventually cross the line from thought into word, and then from word into deed. Sin always begins in our thoughts. *"Above all else, guard your heart (mind), for out of it flow all of the issues of life"* Proverbs 4:23.

God Confronts Job. Job 38:3. *"(God said to Job), 'Brace yourself like a man. I will question you and you shall answer me.'"* God confronts me with this statement every time I read the Bible and every time I listen to a biblical sermon. It is a dangerous thing to study the Bible carefully or attend a church where the minister preaches from the Bible. *"For the Word of God is living and powerful, and sharper than any two edged sword, piercing even to the dividing asunder of soul and spirit, and of the joints and marrow, and is a discerner of the thoughts and intents of the heart"* (Hebrews 4:12). If I don't want the thoughts and intents of my heart discerned, that is, opened up to my own understanding of what they really are, then I better stay away from the Bible and from church. Jesus said, *"This is the verdict: light has come into the world, but men loved darkness instead of light because their deeds were evil"* (John 3 19). The psalmist said, *"Thy word is a lamp unto my feet and a light unto my path"* (Psalm 119:105).

Job's Response. Job 42:5-6. *"My ears had heard of you, but now my eyes have seen you. Therefore I despise myself and repent in dust and ashes."* God revealed his majesty, power and purity to Job. Having seen God, and compared himself to God, Job despised himself and repented. After Isaiah had seen the Lord, he stated, *"Woe to me. I am ruined! I am a man of unclean lips, and I live among a people of unclean lips..."* (Isaiah 6:5a). In the dark, I cannot see how dirty my hands are. But when I turn on the light then I see them in all their filth. Recently I asked a dear friend, a Bible scholar, a saintly man of God in his late 80's, what God had been teaching him in his later years. His immediate answer, "How terribly sinful I really am and how much I need my Savior." If I do not know how sinful I really am, then I must not be very close to God.

Job's Restoration. Job 42:10. *"After Job had prayed for his friends, God made him prosperous again."* Job had been through it all -- loss of family, servants and possessions and then a terribly painful physical affliction. But he had persevered. His faith was intact in spite of a period of deep despair. God had now fully revealed Himself to Job, and Job had confessed and repented. But before restoration, God required Job to do a very humbling thing - pray for and forgive the three 'friends' who had questioned and counseled and slandered him and made him even more miserable. After Job had obeyed, God made him even more prosperous than he had been before his affliction, giving him a large family, servants and many possessions. In the Sermon on the Mount, Jesus stated *"... pray for those who despitefully use you ..."* After confession and repentance, God required this of Job before restoration. Is there anyone out there who has despitefully used me for whom I have not prayed and forgiven? Maybe this is why, even after confession and repentance, I have not yet been fully restored to oneness with God.

Psalms

Throughout the 150 psalms, there are many occasions where the psalmist bears his soul before God and speaks in ways which modern day Christians might question as doubting God's love and faithfulness. But real life is often hard and it is real life where we live. We need to be honest with ourselves and with God. And yet it should be a great encouragement to us to realize that here, in God's Revealed Word, we read, for our instruction and comfort, the cries of despair of real people in real circumstances as well as the joyous praises of thankful hearts.

Except for Psalms 88 and 119, we have selected one or two special verses and quoted it without comment. Psalm 88 and 119 are considered in more detail.

Psalm 1, verse 6. *"For the Lord watches over the way of the righteous, but the way of the wicked shall perish."*

Psalm 2, verse 12b. *"Blessed are all who take refuge in Him."*

Psalm 3, verse 3a. *"You are a shield around me, O Lord."*

Psalm 4, verse 8. *"I will lie down and sleep in peace, for you alone, O Lord, make me dwell in safety."*

Psalm 5, verse 3. *"Morning by morning, O Lord, you hear my voice; morning by morning I lay my requests before you and wait in expectation."*

Psalm 6, verse 9. *"The Lord has heard my cry for mercy; the Lord accepts my prayer."*

Psalm 7, verse 1. *"O Lord my God, I take refuge in you; save me and deliver me from all who pursue me... "*

Psalm 8, verse 1. *"O Lord, our Lord, how majestic is your name in all the earth."*

Psalm 9, verse 16. *"The Lord is known for His justice; the wicked are ensnared by the work of their own hands."*

Psalm 10, verse 17. *"You hear, O Lord, the desire of the afflicted; you encourage them, and listen to their cry. "*

Psalm 11, verse 7. *"The Lord is righteous. He loves justice; upright men will seek his face."*

Psalm 12, verse 6a. *"The words of the Lord are flawless..."*

Psalm 13, verse 5. *"I trust in your unfailing love; my heart rejoices in your salvation."*

Psalm 14, verse 1. *"The fool says in his heart, 'There is no God.'"*

Psalm 15, verse 1, 4b. *"Lord, who may dwell in your sanctuary? Who may dwell in your holy hill? ... He who keeps his promises even when it hurts."*

Psalm 16, verse 8. *"I have set the Lord always before my face. Because He is at my right hand, I will not be shaken."*

Psalm 17, verse 3b. *"I have resolved that my mouth will not sin."*

Psalm 18, verse 28. *"You, O Lord, keep my lamp burning; my God turns my darkness into light."*

Psalm 19, verse 14. *"May the words of my mouth and the meditation of my heart be pleasing to your sight, O Lord, my Rock and my Redeemer."*

Psalm 20, verse 1a. *"May the Lord answer you when you are in distress..."*

Psalm 21, verse 7. *"... the king (commander, leader, supervisor) trusts the Lord; through the unfailing love of the Most High, he (the king) will not be shaken."*

Psalm 22, verse 24. *"For He has not despised or disdained the suffering of the afflicted one; He has not hidden His face from him but has listened to his cry for help."*

Psalm 23, verse 6. *"Surely goodness and love shall follow me all the days of my life and I will dwell in the house of the Lord forever."*

Psalm 24, verse 1. *"The earth is the Lord's and everything in it. The world, and all who live in it."*

Psalm 25, verses 4-5. *"Show me your ways, O Lord, teach me your paths; guide me into your truth and teach me, for you are God my Savior, and my hope is in you all day long."*

Psalm 26, verse 2. *"Test me, O Lord, and try me, examine my heart and my mind."*

Psalm 27, verse 1. *"The Lord is my light and my salvation -- whom shall I fear? The Lord is the stronghold of my life -- of whom shall I be afraid?"*

Psalm 28, verse 27. *"The Lord is my strength and my shield; my heart trusts in Him and I am helped. My heart leaps for joy and I will give thanks to Him in song."*

Psalm 29, verse 11. *"The Lord gives strength to His people; the Lord blesses His people with peace."*

Psalm 30, verse 5b. *"Weeping may remain for a night, but rejoicing comes in the morning."*

Psalm 31, verse 5. *"Into your hands I commit my spirit; redeem me, O Lord, the God of truth."*

Psalm 32, verse 2. *"Blessed is the man whose sin the Lord does not count against Him and in whose spirit there is no deceit."*

Psalm 33, verse 1b. *"The eyes of the Lord are on those who fear Him, on those whose hope is in His unfailing love."*

Psalm 34, verses 4-5. *"I sought the Lord and He answered me; He delivered me from all my fears. Those who look to Him are radiant. Their faces are never covered with shame."*

Psalm 35, verse 28. *"My tongue will speak of your righteousness and of your praises all day long."*

Psalm 36, 1b-2. *"There is no fear of God before their eyes. For in his own eye he flatters himself too much to detect or hate his sin."*

Psalm 37, verse 3. *"Trust in the Lord and do good."*

Psalm 38, verse 5. *"My wounds fester and are loathsome because of my sinful folly."*

Psalm 39, verse 7. *"But now, Lord, what do I look for? My hope is in you."*

Psalm 40, verses 1-4. *"I waited patiently for the Lord; He turned to me and heard my cry. He lifted me out of the slimy pit, out of the mud and mire; He set my feet on a rock and gave me a firm place to stand. He put a new song in my mouth, a hymn of praise to our God. Many will see and put their trust in the Lord. Blessed is the man who makes the Lord his trust."*

Psalm 41, verse 12. *"In my integrity you uphold me and set me in your presence forever.*

Psalm 42, verse 5. *"Why are you downcast, O my soul? Why so disturbed within me? Put your hope in God, for I will yet praise Him, my Savior and my God."*

Psalm 43, verse 3. *"Send forth your light and your truth, let them guide me..."*

Psalm 44, verse 21. *"Would not God have discovered it (my sin), since he knows the secrets of the heart?"*

Psalm 45, verse 1. *"My heart is stirred by a noble theme..."*

Psalm 46, verse 10. *"Be still and know that I am God..."*

Psalm 47, verse 6. *"Sing praises to God, sing praises; sing praises to our King, sing praises."*

Psalm 48, verse 1. *"Great is the Lord, and greatly to be praised."*

Psalm 49, verse 12. *"But man, despite his riches, does not endure; he is like the beasts that perish."*

Psalm 50, verse 15. *"... call upon me in the day of trouble; I will deliver you and you will honor me."*

Psalm 51, verse 6. *"Surely you desire truth in the inner parts; you teach me wisdom in the inmost place."*

Psalm 52, verse 9. *"... in your name will I hope, for your name is good."*

Psalm 53, verse 1. *"The fool says in his heart, 'There is no God.'"*

Psalm 54, verse 2. *"Hear my prayer, O God: listen to the words of my mouth."*

Psalm 55, verses 4-7. *"My heart is in anguish within me; the terrors of death assail me. Fear and trembling have beset me; horror has overwhelmed me. I said, 'O that I had the wings of a dove! I would fly away and be at rest -- I would fly far away...'"*

Psalm 56, verse 3. *When I am afraid, I will trust in You."*

Psalm 57, verse 7. *"My heart is steadfast, O God. My heart is steadfast..."*

Psalm 58, verse 11. *"... Surely the righteous still are rewarded; surely there is a God who judges the earth."*

Psalm 59, verse 17. *"O my Strength, I sing praise to You; You, O God, are my fortress, my loving God."*

Psalm 60, verse 12. **"With God we will gain the victory..."**

Psalm 61, verse 4. *"I long to dwell in your tent forever and take refuge in the shelter of your wings."*

Psalm 62, verse 5-6. *"Find rest, O my soul, in God alone; my hope comes from Him. He alone is my rock and my salvation; he is my fortress. I will not be shaken."*

Psalm 63, verse 3. *"Because your love is better than life, my lips will glorify you."*

Psalm 64, verse 10. *"Let the righteous rejoice in the Lord and take refuge in Him; let all the upright in heart praise Him!"*

Psalm 65, verse 3. *"When we were overwhelmed by sins, you atoned for our transgressions."*

Psalm 66, verse 18. *"If I cherish sin in my heart, the Lord will not listen to me."*

Psalm 67, verse 5. *"May the peoples praise you, O God; may all the peoples praise you."*

Psalm 68, verse 19. *"Praise be to the Lord, to God our Savior, who daily bears our burdens."*

Psalm 69, verse 6. *"May those who hope in you not be disgraced because of me, O Lord, the Lord Almighty; may those who seek you not be put to shame because of me."*

Psalm 70, verse 4. *"May those who seek you rejoice and be glad in you; may those who love your salvation always say, 'Let God be exalted.'"*

Psalm 71, verse 5. *"For you have been my hope, O Sovereign Lord, my confidence since my birth."*

Psalm 72, verse 1-2. (Solomon speaking) - *"Endow (me) with your justice, O God... (and) your righteousness. (I) will (then) judge your people (with) righteousness, your afflicted ones with justice."*

Psalm 73, verse 25-26. *"Whom have I in heaven but you? And being with you, I desire nothing on earth. My flesh and my heart may fail, but God is the strength of my heart and my portion forever."*

Psalm 74, verse 12. *"...You, O God, are my king..."*

Psalm 75, verse 7. *"... It is God who judges..."*

Psalm 76, verse 4. *"You are resplendent with light..."*

Psalm 77, verse 13. *"Your ways, O God, are holy..."*

Psalm 78, verse 72. *"... David shepherded them with integrity of heart; with skillful hands he led them."*

Psalm 79, verse 13. *"... we, the sheep of your pasture, will praise you forever..."*

Psalm 80, verse 19. *"Restore us, O Lord God Almighty; make your face to shine upon us, that we may be saved."*

Psalm 81, verses 9-10. *"You shall have no foreign god among you; you shall not bow down to an alien god. I am the Lord your God..."*

Psalm 82, verse 3. *"Defend the cause of the weak and fatherless; maintain the rights of the poor and oppressed."*

Psalm 83, verse 18. *"Let them know that you, whose name is the Lord, that you alone are the Most High over all the earth."*

Psalm 84, verse 10. *"Better is one day in your courts than a thousand elsewhere; I would rather be a doorkeeper in the house of my God than to dwell in the tents of the wicked."*

Psalm 85, verse 8. *"I will listen to what God the Lord will say; he promises peace to his people, his saints - but let them not return to folly."*

Psalm 86, verse 11. *"Teach me your way, O Lord, and I will walk in your truth; give me an undivided heart that I may fear your name."*

Psalm 87, verse 3, 7. *"Glorious things of thee are spoken ... all my fountains are in you."*

Psalm 88 -- Not all psalms are joyful and upbeat. The same psalmists (the Sons of Korah) who wrote the glowing words in Psalm 87 above also wrote Psalm 88. The words of this psalm ring true in the personal experiences of many, many people.

 + **verse 1.** *"O Lord, the God who saves me, day and night I cry out before you."*

 + **verses 3-9.** *"My soul is full of trouble and my life draws near the grave. I am counted among those who go down to the pit; I am like a man without strength. I am set apart with the dead like the slain who lie in the grave, whom you remember no more, who are cut off from your care. You have put me in the lowest pit, in the darkest depths. Your wrath lies heavily upon me; you have overwhelmed me with all of your waves. You have taken from me my closest friends and have made me repulsive to them. I am confined and cannot escape; my eyes are dim with grief."*

 + **verses 16-18.** *"Your wrath has swept over me; your terrors have destroyed me. All day long they surround me like a flood; they have completely engulfed me.*

You have taken my companions and my loved ones from me; the darkness is my closest friend."

Psalm 89, verses 1, 14. *"I will sing of the love of the Lord forever; with my mouth will I make your faithfulness known through all generations ... Righteousness and justice are the foundation of your throne ..."*

Psalm 90, verse 12. *"Teach us to number our days that we might apply our hearts unto wisdom."*

Psalm 91, verse 1. *"He who dwells in the shelter of the Most High will rest in the shadow of the Almighty."*

Psalm 92, verses 12-15. *"The righteous shall flourish like a palm tree, they will grow like a cedar of Lebanon; planted in the house of the Lord, they will flourish in the courts of our God. They will still bear fruit in old age, they will stay fresh and green, proclaiming, 'The Lord is upright; he is my rock and there is no wickedness in him.'"*

Psalm 93, verse 5. *"Your statutes stand firm; holiness adorns your house for endless days, O Lord."*

Psalm 94, verse 19. *"When anxiety was great within me, your consolation brought joy to my soul."*

Psalm 95, verses 7-8. *"...Today, if you hear his voice, do not harden your heart..."*

Psalm 96, verse 9. *"Worship the Lord in the splendor of his holiness; tremble before him, all the earth."*

Psalm 97, verse 10. *"Let those who love the Lord hate evil..."*

Psalm 98, verse 4. *"Shout for joy to the Lord, all the earth, burst into jubilant song..."*

Psalm 99, verse 5. *"Exalt the Lord our God and worship at his footstool; he is holy."*

Psalm 100, verses 4-5. *"Enter his gates with thanksgiving, and his courts with praise; give thanks unto him and bless his name. For the Lord is good and his love endures forever; his faithfulness continues through all generations."*

Psalm 101, verse 3. *"I will set before my eyes no vile thing."*

Psalm 102, verses 1-2. *Hear my prayer, O Lord; let my cry for help come to you. Do not hide your face from me when I am in distress."*

Psalm 103, verses 11-12. *"For as high as the heavens are above the earth, so great is His love for those who fear Him. As far as the east is from the west, so far has He removed our transgressions from us."*

Psalm 104, verses 33-34. *"I will sing to the Lord all my life; I will sing praise to my God as long as I live. May my meditation be pleasing to Him, as I rejoice in the Lord."*

Psalm 105, verses 3-4. *"Glory in His holy name; let the hearts of those who seek the Lord rejoice. Look to God and to His strength; seek His face always."*

Psalm 106, verse 3. *"Blessed are they who maintain justice, who constantly do what is right."*

Psalm 107, verses 2, 14, 20-21. *"Let the redeemed of the Lord (be bold and speak up) ... for He brought them out of darkness and the deepest gloom and broke away their chains ... He sent forth His word and healed them; he rescued them from the grave. Let them give thanks to the Lord for his unfailing love and His wonderful deeds for men."*

Psalm 108, verse 1. *"My heart is steadfast, O God. I will sing and make music with all my soul."*

Psalm 109, verse 27. *"Let them know that it was your hand, that you, O Lord, have done it."*

Psalm 110, verse 5. *"The Lord is at your right hand..."*

Psalm 111, verse 10. *"The fear of the Lord is the beginning of wisdom; all who follow His precepts have good understanding..."*

Psalm 112, verses 4, 7 *"Even in darkness light dawns for the upright, for the gracious and compassionate and righteous man ... He will have no fear of bad news; his heart is steadfast, trusting in the Lord."*

Psalm 113, verse 3. *"From the rising of the sun to the place where it sets, the name of the Lord is to be praised."*

Psalm 114, verse 8. *"Tremble, O earth, in the presence of the Lord..."*

Psalm 115, verse 1. *"Not to us, O Lord, not to us, but to your name be the glory, because of your love and faithfulness."*

Psalm 116, verse 15. *"Precious in the sight of the Lord is the death of Hs saints."*

Psalm 117, verse 2. *"...Praise the Lord."*

Psalm 118, verse 6, 8, 14, 24. *"The Lord is with me; I will not be afraid. What can man do to me? ... It is better to take refuge in the Lord than to trust in man ... The Lord is my strength and my song; He is my salvation ... This is the day the Lord has made; let us rejoice and be glad in it."*

Psalm 119 -- Psalm 119 is the longest Psalm, containing 176 verses. It is also the longest chapter in the Bible. In almost every verse there is a specific reference to God's Law, our Bible. Look for words such as precepts, commands, statutes, ways, decrees, word, commandments and promise. All are synonyms for God's Law.

+ **Verse 2.** *"Blessed are they who keep his statutes and seek Him with all their heart."*

+ **Verse 9.** *"How can a young man keep his way pure? By living according to your word."*

+ **Verse 11.** *"I have hidden your word in my heart (memorized it) so that I might not sin against you."*

+ **Verse 14.** *"I rejoice in following your statutes as one rejoices in great riches."*

+ **Verse 18.** *"Open my eyes that I may see wonderful things in your law."*

+ **Verse 24.** *"Your statutes are my delight; they are my counselors (advisors)."*

+ **Verse 30.** *"I have chosen the way of truth; I have set my heart on your laws."*

+ **Verse 32.** *"I run in the path of your commands, for they have set my heart free."*

+ **Verse 36.** *"Turn my heart toward your statutes and not toward selfish gain."*

+ **Verse 37.** *"Turn my eyes away from worthless things; renew my life according to your word."*

+ **Verse 45.** *"I will walk about in freedom, for I have sought your precepts."*

+ **Verse 72.** *"The law from your mouth is more precious to me than thousands of pieces of silver and gold."*

+ **Verse 92.** *"If your law had not been my delight, I would have perished in my affliction."*

+ **Verses 99.** *"I have more insight than all my teachers (pagan college professors?) for I meditate on your statutes.*

+ **Verse 105.** *"Your word is a lamp to my feet and a light for my path."*

+ **Verse 111.** *Your statutes are my heritage forever; they are the joy of my heart."*

+ **Verse 112.** *"My heart is set on keeping your decrees to the very end."*

+ **Verse 130.** *"The entrance of your words give light; they give understanding to the simple (uninformed)."*

+ **Verse 133.** *"Direct my footsteps according to your word; let no sin rule over me."*

+ **Verse 160.** *"All your words are true; all your righteous laws are eternal."*

+ **Verse 165.** *"Great peace have they who love your law, and nothing can make them stumble."*

+ Verse 167. *"I obey your statutes for I love them greatly."*

+ Verse 169. *"May my cry come before you, O God: give me understanding according to your word."*

Psalm 120, verse 2. *"Save me, Lord, from lying lips and from deceitful tongues."*

Psalm 121, verses 1-2. *"I lift up my eyes to the hills. Does my help come from them? No, my help comes from the Lord, the Maker of heaven and earth.*

Psalm 122, verse 1. *"I rejoiced with those who said to me, 'Let us go to the house of the Lord.'"*

Psalm 123, verses 3-4. *"Have mercy on us, O Lord, have mercy on us, for we have endured much contempt. We have endured much ridicule from the proud, much contempt from the arrogant."*

Psalm 124, verse 8. *"Our help is in the name of the Lord, the Maker of heaven and earth."*

Psalm 125, verse 2. *"As the mountains surround Jerusalem, so the Lord surrounds his people both now and forevermore."*

Psalm 126, verse 3. *"The Lord has done great things for us and we are filled with joy."*

Psalm 127, verse 1. *"Unless the Lord builds the house, its builders labor in vain."*

Psalm 128, verses 1-2. *"Blessed are all who fear the Lord, who walk in His ways. You will eat the fruit of your labor, blessings and prosperity will be yours.*

Psalm 129, verse 4. *"The Lord is righteous. He has cut me free from the bonds of the wicked."*

Psalm 130, verses 3-4. *"If you, O Lord, kept a record of sins, no one could stand. But with you there is forgiveness; therefore you are feared."*

Psalm 131, verses 1-2. *"My heart is not proud, O Lord, my eyes are not haughty ... I have stilled and quieted my soul..."*

Psalm 132, verse 9. *"May our spiritual leaders be clothed with righteousness; may we all sing with joy."*

Psalm 133, verse 1. *"How good and pleasant it is when brothers live together in unity!"*

Psalm 134, verse 1. *"Praise the Lord, all of you who are servants of the Lord."*

Psalm 135, verses 15-18. *"The idols of the nations are silver and gold, made by the hands of men. They have mouths but cannot speak, eyes but cannot see; they have ears but cannot hear, nor is there breath in their mouths. Those who make them will be like them, and so will those who trust in them."* -- We become like the things that we worship.

Psalm 136, verse 26. *"Give thanks to the Lord of heaven. His love endures forever."*

Psalm 137, verse 4. *"How can we sing the songs of the Lord when we are in a foreign land?"* -- When we are far from God, we cannot sing the songs of praise and hope. Only as we return to our Lord will our hearts be able to sing His praises again.

Psalm 138, verse 3. *"When I called, you answered me; you made me bold and stouthearted."*

Psalm 139, verses 1-4, 14, 23-24. *"O Lord, you have searched me and you know me. You know when I sit and when I rise; you perceive my thoughts from afar. You discern my going out and my lying down; you are familiar with all my ways. Before a word is on my tongue you know it completely, O Lord... I praise you because I am fearfully and wonderfully made... Search me, O God, and know my heart; test me and know my anxious thoughts. See if there is any offensive way in me, and lead me into the way everlasting."*

Psalm 140, verses 12-13. *"I know that the Lord secures justice for the poor and upholds the cause of the needy. Surely the righteous* (those who do the same) *will praise your name and the upright will live before you."*

Psalm 141, verse 4. *"Let not my heart be drawn to what is evil."* -- If we are not seeking what is good, we will slide toward what is evil.

Psalm 142, verses 6-7. *"Listen to my cry for I am in desperate need ... set me free from my prison* (from the sin which has entangled me) *that I may praise your name."*

Psalm 143, verses 6, 8, 10. *"My soul thirsts for you like a parched land ... Let the morning bring me word of your unfailing love for I have put my trust in you ... Teach me to do your will, for you are my God, may your Spirit lead me on level ground."*

Psalm 144, verse 1. *"Praise be to the Lord, my Rock, who trains my hands for war and my fingers for battle."*

Psalm 145, verse 18. *"The Lord is near to all who call upon him, to all who call on him in truth."*

Psalm 146, verse 5. *"Blessed is he whose help is the God of Jacob, whose hope is in the Lord his God."*

Psalm 147, verse 11. *"The Lord delights in those who fear him, who put their hope in His unfailing love."*

Psalm 148, verse 13. *"Let them praise the name of the Lord, for his name alone is exalted; his splendor is above the earth and heavens."*

Psalm 149, verses 3-4. *"Let them praise his name with dancing and make music to him with tambourine and harp. For the Lord takes delight in his people; he crowns the humble with salvation."*

Psalm 150, verse 6. *"Let everything that hath breath praise the Lord. Praise the Lord."*

The Psalms begin with *"Blessed is the man,"* and end with *"Praise the Lord."*

Proverbs

Every proverb is a "nugget of gold." They are all written by Solomon, except for chapter 30 (Sayings of Agur) and chapter 31 (Sayings of King Lemuel). The proverbs are practical guides to daily, godly living. Samples have been selected from each chapter. For some, comments are offered.

Chapter 1, verses 1-4, 10. *"The proverbs of Solomon, son of David, king of Israel: for attaining wisdom and discipline, for understanding words of insight, for acquiring a disciplined and prudent life, doing what is right and just and fair; for giving prudence to the uninstructed, knowledge and discretion to the young ... The fear of the Lord is the beginning of wisdom."*

Chapter 2, verse 6. *"For the Lord gives wisdom, from His mouth come knowledge and understanding."*

Chapter 3, verses 3, 5-6, 27. *"Let love and faithfulness never leave you; bind them around your neck, write them on the table of your heart ... Trust in the Lord with all your heart and lean not unto your own understanding; in all your ways acknowledge Him, and He will direct your path ... do not withhold good from those who deserve it, when it is within your power to act."*

Chapter 4, verse 23. *"Above all else, guard your heart, for it is the wellspring of life."*

Chapter 5, verses 18-19. *"...may you rejoice in the wife of your youth. A loving doe, a graceful deer -- may her breasts satisfy you always, may you ever be captivated by her love."*

Chapter 6, verses 20-21. *"My son, keep your father's commands and do not forsake your mother's teaching. Bind them on your heart forever..."*

Chapter 7, verses 24-27. *"Now then, my sons, listen to me; pay attention to what I say. Do not let your heart turn to the ways of the sexually immoral woman or stray into her paths. Many are the victims she has brought down; her slain are a mighty throng. Her house is a highway to the grave, leading down to the chambers of death."*

Chapter 8, verses 7, 20. *"My mouth speaks what is true, for my lips detest* *wickedness ... I walk in the way of righteousness, along the paths of justice."*

Chapter 9, verse 10. *"The fear of the Lord is the beginning of wisdom, and knowledge of the Holy one is understanding."*

Chapter 10, verse 9. *"The man of integrity walks securely, but he who takes crooked paths will be found out."*

Chapter 11, verses 2, 25. *"When pride comes, then comes disgrace, but with humility comes wisdom... A generous man will prosper; he who refreshes others will himself be refreshed."* Paul said to Philemon (Philemon, verse 6), *"You have given me great joy and encouragement, because you, brother, have refreshed the hearts of the saints."* Does my presence refresh the hearts of my family, my friends, my coworkers?

Chapter 12, verse 25. *"An anxious heart weighs a man down, but a kind word cheers him up."* We have a small fabric wall hanging in our kitchen which states: "Look up, and laugh, and love, and lift." Everyone is weighed down to some extent by an anxious heart. Everyone needs a kind word to cheer him up.

Chapter 13, verse 20. *"He who walks with the wise becomes wise, but a companion of fools suffers harm."* Parents, are you selecting the right friends for your young children?

Chapter 14, verse 15. *"A simple man believes anything, but a prudent man gives thoughts to his steps."* Naivety is not a virtue. We are to be *"wise as serpents, but as harmless as doves."*

Chapter 15, verses 1, 28. *"A gentle word turns away wrath, but a harsh word stirs up anger ... The heart of the righteous weighs its answers."*

Chapter 16, verse 18. *"Pride goes before destruction, a haughty spirit before a fall."* Why? Because pride is a rejection of reality, and nothing succeeds unless it conforms to reality.

Chapter 17, verse 12. *"A cheerful heart is a good medicine. But a crushed spirit dries up the bones."* Recent valid medical research is now confirming what God has been telling us for thousands of years.

Chapter 18, verse 19. *"An offended brother is more unyielding than a fortified* *city, and disputes are like the barred gates of a citadel."* Unfortunate, but true. Jesus set the ultimate standard. *"Father forgive them for they know not what they do ... forgive not seven times seven, but seventy times seven."* True forgiveness is rare - even among Christians.

Chapter 19, verse 20. *"Listen to advice and accept instruction and in the end you will be wise."*

Chapter 20, verse 22. *"Do not say, 'I'll pay you back for this wrong.' Wait for the Lord and He will deliver you."* Do I really trust God to do this? Or does He need my help?

Chapter 21, verses 3, 21. *"To do what is right and just is more acceptable to the Lord than sacrifice ... He who pursues righteousness and love finds life, prosperity and honor."* In both the Old and New Testaments, God speaks of those things which bring Him honor. Boiled down, they are justice (righteousness), mercy (love), and faithfulness (keeping your mind and heart and walk focused on God). Micah 6:8 states, *"...And what doth the Lord require of you but to do justly, to love mercy, and to walk humbly with God."*

Chapter 22, verse 3. *"A prudent man sees danger and takes refuge, but the simple (uninformed) keep going and suffer for it."* Joseph saw a famine coming in Egypt and stored up grain each year to feed the people when the famine came. Nehemiah recognized the external opposition he was facing in rebuilding the walls of Jerusalem and posted armed guards all along the wall. Jesus spoke of a wise builder counting the cost of a new house before he started building it. Faith does not mean acting foolishly and assuming that God will rescue you from an evident danger for which you have not adequately prepared.

Chapter 23, verses 20, 29-33. *"Do not join those who drink too much wine ... Who has woe? Who has sorrow? Who has strife? Who has needless bruises? Who has bloodshot eyes? Those who linger over wine... In the end it bites like a snake, and poisons like a viper. Your eyes will see strange sights and your mind imagine confusing things."* The Bible does not prohibit the drinking of alcoholic beverages. But it does get very explicit regarding the danger of drinking too much. The first effect of alcohol is to weaken a person's moral inhibitions. He (or she) still knows what is right and wrong, but the commitment to do right fades rapidly after a couple of beers or a glass of wine, and the person's attitude becomes one of, "So what? Who cares? No big deal. I will do it anyway." This is especially true in the realm of sexual temptation.

Chapter 24, verse 19. *"Do not fret because of evil men or be envious of the wicked."* Too much time is wasted in fretting and envy. It is far better to plow ahead in productive, positive effort.

Chapter 25, verse 26. *"Like a muddied spring or a polluted well is a righteous man who gives way wickedness."* A college freshman succumbed to sexual temptation at a fraternity party. Describing his reaction, he stated that after it was over he felt dirty, polluted, defiled. He couldn't get rid of the sense of having done something vile and lost something very valuable.

Chapter 26, verses 23-25. *"Like a coating of glaze over earthenware are fervent lips with an evil heart. A malicious man disguises himself with his lips, but in his heart he harbors deceit. Though his speech is charming, do not believe him..."* Do not judge a person's character by the words he speaks. Jesus called the Pharisees *"white washed tomb stones, full of dead men's bones."* Look at a person's whole life. Of what does it truly consist? Is he worth emulating?

Chapter 27, verse 2. *"Let another praise you, and not your own mouth, someone else and not your own lips."* The best praise we can ever get is the inner satisfaction of knowing that we have done the right thing and thus pleased God.

Chapter 28, verse 1. *"The wicked man flees though no one pursues, but the righteous are as bold as a lion."* It is guilt, and the fear of being caught, which causes a man to flee even though no one yet knows what he has done. The righteous man knows that he is not guilty, and stands firm.

Chapter 29, verses 4, 14. *"By justice a king (commander) gives a country (unit) stability ... If a king (commander) judges the poor (his soldiers) with fairness, his throne (command) will always be secure."* A commander's moral weakness encourages mischief. A commander's moral strength encourages righteousness and diligence.

Chapter 30, verses 5-6. *"Every word of God is flawless; he is a shield to those who take refuge in Him. Do not add to his words or He will rebuke you and prove you a liar."* There is a warning here to be accurate in teaching or speaking God's word. Paul says that you should, *"study to make yourself approved unto God, a workman who needs not to be ashamed, rightly dividing (understanding in depth) the Word of Truth."* (2 Timothy 2:15)

Chapter 31, Verses 8-9. Proverbs 31 is known for its famous epilogue (verses 10-31) which describes the wife of noble character. But verses 1-9 are also significant. They contain the advice given to King Lemuel by his mother. Verses 8-9 read: *"Speak up for those who cannot speak for themselves, for the rights of all those who are destitute. Speak up and judge fairly; defend the rights of the poor and needy."* A good leader will be the spokesman for his soldiers to the higher echelons of command. The common soldiers simply cannot speak for themselves. This is their commander's duty. He needs to make sure that the needs of his soldiers and their families are properly reflected in the policies and plans of the higher command.

Ecclesiastes

When Solomon became King of Israel replacing his father David, the magnificent warrior-poet, he asked God for wisdom and discernment so that he could rule the people fairly and compassionately. God granted Solomon's request, and ever since, Solomon has been known as the wisest of all men.

Solomon wrote most of the book of Proverbs, each of which is a pithy statement of how to live each day in a manner pleasing to God.

Solomon also wrote Ecclesiastes, a deeply moving theological treatise on the fleeting nature of life and the utter meaninglessness of a life lived without God as its focus. In Ecclesiastes, Solomon presents the secular, pagan world view for what it really is - meaningless, vain, fleeting.

Someone has said that the highest achievement of human reason is the recognition that there is a limit to human reason. God has said, *"For my ways are not your ways and my thoughts are higher than your thoughts."* Faith is believing and living in that realm of spiritual understanding which is beyond human reason and understanding.

There are many, many Christians who are living in the murky, frightening shadows of agnosticism, hoping that the Christian faith is real, but deep down are haunted because, according to their own human reason and understanding, it just doesn't make sense. How can one reconcile the tragedies of life - disease, pain, suffering, sorrow, natural disasters, famine, poverty and war - with a "good" God? Solomon warns us of this fallacious thinking in Proverbs 3:5-6, *"Trust the Lord with all your heart and lean not on your own understanding."* For the pagan, seeing is believing. For the Christian, believing is seeing.

In Ecclesiastes, Solomon, the wisest of all men, lays bare the emptiness of the secular, pagan world view and enjoins us to live in that spiritual realm where trusting God and obeying Him is the only viable intellectual and practical option.

The End of the Matter. Chapter 1, verse 2. *"Meaningless, meaningless! says the Teacher. Utterly meaningless! Everything is meaningless."* Solomon is referring to himself when he uses the term 'Teacher'. Throughout Ecclesiastes, the word 'meaningless' (the King James uses the word 'vanity') can be translated as 'fleeting,' passing away, without permanence, having no real and enduring value.

When Solomon looks at the past, the present and the future, he sees nothing which is permanent. Therefore, everything is 'meaningless, having no enduring value.' However, at the end of the book, in summing up all wisdom, Solomon states: *"Now all has been heard; here is the conclusion to the matter. Fear God and keep his commandments, for this is the whole duty of man."* (Chapter 12, verse 13)

Getting or Giving. Chapter 2, verses 4-11. *"I undertook great projects: I built houses for myself and planted vineyards. I made gardens and parks and planted all kinds of fruit trees in them. I made reservoirs to water groves of flourishing trees... I also owned more herds and flocks than anyone in Jerusalem before me. I amassed silver and gold for myself... I acquired men and women singers and a harem as well -- the delights of the heart of man... I denied myself nothing my eyes desired. I refused my heart no pleasure... Yet when I surveyed all that my hands had done and what I had toiled to achieve, everything was meaningless (fleeting), a chasing after the wind; nothing was gained under the sun."* The pagan, secular world view is to get everything possible for our own pleasure. In the end, it is meaningless. It is a biblical principle that giving is far better than receiving. Lord help me to be a believing, giving person, not a pagan, getting person.

From the Hand of God. Chapter 2, verses 24-25. *"A man can do nothing better than to eat and drink and find satisfaction in his work. This too, I see, is from the hand of God; for without Him, who can eat or find any enjoyment."* Solomon makes this statement in one form or another several places in Ecclesiastes (3:13, 3:22, 5:18, 8:15, 9:7). The pagan world has picked up on this and twisted it to mean, "Eat, drink and be merry, for tomorrow you may die." This is not what Solomon is saying. Solomon is saying that all of the striving for wealth, position and power is meaningless - fleeting. It is "a chasing after the wind." In the long run, it means nothing because it will not endure. What truly has worth is to enjoy the life God has given us, and to do good. *"I know that there is nothing better for men than to be happy and to do good while they live."* (Chapter 3, verse 12)

Eventually, Everything Will Happen. Chapter 3, verses 1 - 8. (beginning with) *"There is a time for everything and a season for every activity under heaven; a time to be born, and a time to die..."* (and ending with) *"a time for war and a time for peace."* Solomon's "everything" and "every activity" is wholly inclusive. It doesn't leave out anything - even ungodly behavior prohibited elsewhere in the Bible. So is there an inconsistency here? No, not really. By stating that there is a *"time for everything"* Solomon is not pronouncing moral judgment. He is not saying that EVERYTHING is morally right in its time (although some people try to justify their ungodly lifestyle by referring to this passage.) Solomon is simply stating the obvious truth that during the course of time, everything - both good and bad - will eventually take place. Solomon is not justifying any of these activities. He is saying that, over a period of time, all of these things will happen. This is in the context of his teaching on the fleeting nature of life, and the absolute meaninglessness of trying to live without God.

The Price of Folly. Chapter 10, verse 1. *"As dead flies give perfume a bad smell, so a little folly outweighs wisdom and honor."* Solomon expressed a similar truth when he stated in Proverbs, chapter 25, verse 26, *"Like a muddied spring or a polluted well is a righteous man who gives way to wickedness."* It is sad but true that a person can live a spotless, righteous life for decades and then, because of one serious indiscretion, he or she will be remembered by that indiscretion. Shakespeare wrote, "The evil (that) men do lives after them. The good is oft interred with their bones."

Wisdom Beyond Human Understanding. Chapter 8, verse 17. *"... No one can comprehend what goes on under the sun. Despite all his efforts to search it out, man cannot discover its meaning. Even if a wise man claims he knows, he cannot really comprehend it."* This statement validates the wisdom of Solomon. He realized that there is a wisdom beyond human understanding. When a person finally grasps this truth, then the way is clear for that "leap of faith" into the spiritual world of God's thoughts about true reality as expressed in the Bible, the Word of God.

Begin Young and Enjoy God All of Your Life. Chapter 12, verse 1. *"Remember your Creator in the days of your youth, before the days of trouble come and the years approach when you will say, 'I find no pleasure in them.'"* Solomon is stating that we should start enjoying God early in life and not wait until old age. Although the deathbed conversion of an elderly loved one brings great joy, it is clouded by the realization that a whole life lived without God is a horrible experience. It is the wise young person who realizes that the world of sin offers no pleasure comparable to the overwhelming joy of living life in the company of the Living God.

The End of the Matter. Chapter 12, verses 13-14. *"Now all has been heard; here is the conclusion of the matter. Fear God and keep His commandments for this is the whole duty of man. For God will bring every deed into judgment, including every hidden thing, whether it be good or evil."* Knowing this, how should I then live? What changes do I need to make in my life?

Song of Solomon

This is the third of the three books of the Bible written by Solomon, King of Israel, son of David. Halley's Bible Handbook states, "It is a Love Song, set in blossoming springtime, abounding in metaphors and a profusion of oriental imagery ..."

This book has been criticized, and its place in the canon challenged, because of its amorous language. Some biblical scholars believe that it as an allegorical description of the relationship between God and his Chosen People, or of Christ and His Church. And this may be so.

However, the Song of Solomon may well be exactly what it sounds like -- a celebration of the sexual relationship between a man and woman in marriage. Halley states, "Its essence is to be found in its tender and devoted expressions of the intimate delights of wedded love." The powerful and moving lyrics describe, by exquisite imagery, what God intends to be a beautiful, intimate, loving and exciting relationship between a husband and wife.

Below are a few passages from the Song of Solomon along with possible interpretations. Scripture references are quoted from The New International Version (NIV). We suggest reading it also in other translations, e.g., the King James Version, the Revised Standard Version, The New Living Bible from Tyndale House, "The Message" by Eugene Peterson, and then interpreting the meaning of this poem for yourself.

There are two primary "speakers" in the Song of Solomon.
   > The first is the husband - the "lover", the active giver and initiator of love.
   > The second is the wife - the "beloved", the enthusiastic receiver of her husband's love.

Chapter 1

   > **Wife: (verse 1)** - *"Let him kiss me with the kisses of his mouth - for your love is more delightful than wine."* I am intoxicated by your love.

   > **Husband: (verse 15)** - *"How beautiful you are, my darling! Oh how beautiful."* I am overwhelmed by your beauty.

> **Wife: (verse 16)** - *"How handsome you are, my lover! Oh, how charming! And our bed is verdant."* Our 'bed', the sexual aspect of our relationship, is lush and fertile.

> **Husband: (verse 17)** - *"The beams of our house are cedars; our rafters are firs."* Our 'house' is our marriage, and it is strong, secure, permanent and ordained by God.

Chapter 2

> **Husband: (verse 2)** - *"Like a lily among thorns is my darling among the maidens."* Among all women, she is uniquely beautiful and lovely, invoking the idea of 'forsaking all others.'

> **Wife: (verse 3a)** - *"Like an apple tree among the trees of the forest is my lover among the young men."* Among all men, he is uniquely manly and virile, again invoking the idea of 'forsaking all others.'

> **Wife: (verse 3b)** - *"I delight to sit in his shade, and his fruit is sweet to my taste."* I have no desire other than to be with him and to go wherever he goes, all of my life. I will find my full contentment in sharing in his life as his helpmeet and companion.

> **Wife: (verse 4)** - *"He has taken me to the banquet hall, and his banner over me is love."* As I look ahead at our life together, what I see is good and beautiful - a continuing banquet. I am secure in his love for me because it is for me and me alone.

> **Wife: (verse 6)** - *"His left arm is under my head and his right arm embraces me."* My head is cradled in his left arm. He is caressing and exploring my body with his right hand.

> **Wife: (verse 7)** - *"Daughters of Jerusalem, I charge you... Do not arouse or awaken love until it so desires."* A message to unmarried young women. Do not play around or experiment with your sexuality. Do not allow yourself to become aroused until the time has come when, in the freedom and holiness of the marriage relationship, you can, in good conscience and with complete abandon, go 'all the way'. This same admonition is also found in chapter 3, verse 5; and chapter 8, verse 4. Thus it has special significance.

> **Wife: (verse 8)** - *"Listen! It is my lover. Look! Here he comes, leaping over the mountains, bounding over the hills."* He is turning toward me. I am excited beyond all expectation. We are together.

> **Husband: (verse 10)** - *"... Arise, my darling, my beautiful one, and come with me."* Come to me, my beloved wife. Embrace me fully.

> **Wife: (verse 16a)** - *"My lover is mine and I am his..."* He is in me. We are one flesh. I am complete.

Chapter 4, verses 1-15; Chapter 5, verses 10-16; Chapter 6, verses 4-12; Chapter 7, verses 1-9. In these passages, the husband and wife revel unashamedly in the beauty and grace of each other's bodies.

Chapter 4, Wife: (verse 16b). *"Let my lover come into my garden and taste of its choice fruits."* Come, my husband, and let us make love again.

Chapter 5, Husband: (verse 1). *"I have come into my garden, my bride ... I have gathered my myrrh with my spice. I have eaten my honeycomb and my honey; I have drunk my wine and my milk."* I have responded to your invitation to make love again and I am satiated by the experience.

Chapter 6, Wife: (Verse 3). *"I am my lover's and my lover is mine."* We are secure in a beautiful marriage relationship which God both ordained and affirms - a relationship consisting of one man and one woman, committed to each other in marriage, until death do us part.

Chapter 8, verses 6b-7a. *"... love (sexual desire) is as strong as death, its ardor as unyielding as the grave. It burns like blazing fire, like a mighty flame. Many waters cannot quench love; rivers cannot wash it away."* - Sexual desire is a basic instinct, imbedded in every human being by God's design, both for the propagation of the race and for the fulfillment of unity in marriage. Sexual desire is there in every person, and it cannot be extinguished or quenched or washed away. But it is not to be aroused before "it's time," which means in marriage. Sex is to be confined within the boundaries of a secure, permanent, faithful marriage where frequent consummation is not only biblically authorized but also commanded. It is only in the freedom and security of marriage that the sexual relationship between a man and a woman can be experienced in its true beauty, its unimaginable excitement, and its full and lasting satisfaction.

The Major Prophets

Isaiah, Jeremiah, Lamentations, Ezekiel and Daniel

Halley's Bible Handbook states:

> The Historical Books of the Old Testament, Genesis through Esther, are the story of the Rise and Fall of the Hebrew Nation.

> The Poetical Books, Job through Song of Solomon, roughly belong to the Golden Age of the Hebrew Nation.

> The Prophetical Books, Isaiah to Malachi, belong to the days of the (Decline and) Fall of the Hebrew Nation.

Old Testament Prophets did the following:

> They "forth-told" - they set forth boldly and publicly the current truth about the moral and spiritual condition of the Hebrew people.

> They "fore-told" - they proclaimed the future consequences of both good and evil conduct.

> Some of the prophets provided insights into God's plans for the future, to include the end times.

Isaiah

Stop Doing Wrong, Start Doing Right. Chapter 1, verses 5a,13, 16-17, 19-20. *"...Why do you persist in rebellion? ... (the Lord says) 'Stop bringing meaningless offerings to me ... (instead) wash and make yourselves clean. Take your evil deeds out of my sight! Stop doing wrong, learn to do right! Seek justice. Encourage the oppressed. Defend the cause of the fatherless, plead the case of the widow ... If you are willing and obedient, you will eat the best from the land, but if you resist and rebel, you will be devoured by the sword.'"* Isaiah lived during the era of the kings of Judah and Israel, about 250 years after Solomon and 750 years before Christ. Isaiah looked around and took stock of the condition of God's chosen people. He saw that they had fallen into terrible spiritual and moral depravity. Isaiah proclaimed their sins from the rooftops, but he also proclaimed a way out, and it was the way of confession, repentance and turning back to God. In reading the Old Testament, one cannot help but be appalled at the evil of the Hebrew people and the sordid lifestyle of some of the Old Testament 'saints.' But we can also be deeply encouraged that God never let them go. Having chosen the Israelites as His own special people, He put up with their sins to bring them to Himself and make of them a people who would bring glory and honor to His name. He was not happy about their conduct. But He was faithful to them and continued to love them - like good parents of an errant child. Fortunately for us all, He is the same today.

The Unvarnished Truth. Chapter 1, verses 21a-23, 25, 27-28. *"See how the faithful city (Jerusalem) has become a harlot! She was once full of justice; righteousness used to dwell in her - but now murderers! Your silver has become dross, your choice wine is diluted with water ... Your rulers are rebels, companions of thieves; they all love bribes and chase after gifts. They do not defend the cause of the fatherless, the widow's case does not come before them... I will thoroughly purge away your dross and remove your impurities ... Zion (Jerusalem) will be redeemed with justice, her penitent ones with righteousness. But rebels and sinners will both be broken together, and those who forsake the Lord will perish."* We could substitute modern day Washington, DC, for Jerusalem in this passage. God will not be mocked. There will be a day of judgment for our nation. Will I be found among the penitent ones? -- or among the rebels and sinners who have forsaken the Lord?

The Reward of Doing What Is Right. Chapter 3, verse 10. *"Tell the righteous it will be well with them, for they will enjoy the fruit of their deeds."* The Old

Testament is not all 'gloom and doom.' For those who seek to do what is right in accordance with biblical standards, there is the promise of a joyful reward.

A Call for Honesty. Chapter 5, verse 20a. *"Woe to those who call evil good and good evil..."* It started with Satan when he told Eve that what God had called evil was really not evil but was actually good. And it continues on to this day, in a thousand different forms. The Bible states what is good and what is evil. We, then, have the responsibility of finding out by studying the Bible what is good and adhering to the good. And we have the responsibility of calling good good, and evil evil, and not watering down the truth.

Stand Firm in Your Faith. Chapter 7, verse 9. *"If you do not stand firm in your faith, you will not stand at all."* Hebrews 11:1 states that faith is, *"being sure of what you hope for and certain of what you cannot see."* When everything goes wrong or life seems to be without meaning, we must hang on to what we hope for but cannot see -- the biblical promise of the presence of the Lord Jesus Christ in our lives. If we stand on that promise as fact, God will reveal Himself to us in power and clarity and joy. But if we do not, we will surely fall into fear, confusion and despair.

Unjust and Unnecessary Requirements. Chapter 10, verse 1. *"Woe to those who make unjust laws, to those who issue oppressive decrees."* Whatever our situation, we are constantly imposing rules, both ourselves and others. The question is, 'Are these rules biblical?' What rules have I set for my life? Are they so difficult as to be impossible of achievement, making me miserable, devoid of joy, humor, and hope? Or - maybe my rules for myself are so lax and fluid that I permit almost anything, and end up without zeal for God or purpose in life? Do I hold others (my spouse, my children, my friends, my coworkers, subordinates, my students) to standards of performance which are so demanding, rigid, harsh, and oppressive that they become discouraged thus lose any desire to achieve? Micah 6:8 states, *"What doth the Lord require of thee but to do justly, to love mercy and to walk humbly with God."* Do my rules for myself and others reflect justice, mercy and faithfulness?

Perfect Peace. Chapter 26, verse 3. *"Thou wilt keep him in perfect peace whose mind is stayed on thee..."* (KJV). Peace! The absence of conflict, anxiety, tension, anger, bitterness, and stress. Are you at peace with God, with yourself, with your family and friends? You CAN be! Focus your mind and heart on God and He will give you peace, described by Jesus as the *"peace which is beyond understanding."*

False Worship. Chapter 29, verse 13. *"The Lord says, 'These people ... honor me with their lips, but their hearts are far from me. Their worship of me is made up only of rules taught by men.'"* Personalize this and see if it fits. "I honor You with my lips, but my heart is far from You. My worship of You is made up only of rules made by men." Are you just going through the motions in your worship? Where is your heart when your mind is in neutral? True worship, according to the Word of God, is in *"spirit and in truth."* That means allowing God's Spirit to lead you into all Truth about Himself, about your world, about yourself.

The Ultimate Confrontation. Chapter 30, verses 10-11. *"They say ... to the prophets (preachers) ... 'Tell us pleasant things ... stop confronting us with the Holy one of Israel.'"* Jesus stated that people will not come to the light because their deeds are evil (John 3:18). The Apostle Paul stated that Christians are a stench in the nostrils of sinners (2 Cor. 2:16). No one wants their sins to be revealed. But that is what happens when a person is confronted with the Holy One of Israel. Christians are called to be witnesses - to include confronting people with the fact of God.

Repentance. Chapter 30, verse 15. *"This is what ... the Holy One of Israel says: 'In repentance ... is your salvation ...'"* John the Baptist began his ministry with a call to repentance. Jesus began His ministry with a call to repentance. Repentance begins with recognition of sin and confession. Do Christians sin? 1 John 1:8 states, *"If we claim to be without sin, we deceive ourselves and the truth is not in us."* And, take note, the Apostle John was writing to Christians. We constantly sin - by thoughts, words and deeds, both in commission and omission. Read the Bible and compare your life with the Holy One of Israel. Every thinking Christian recognizes his sin every time he reads the Bible, because in the Bible the reader is confronted with holiness. But recognition and confession is not enough. There must be repentance - a genuine turning away from sin - before there can be restoration of fellowship with God.

Do Right, Gain Peace. Chapter 32, verse 17. *"The fruit of righteousness will be peace..."* Righteousness means doing what is just, doing what is good. In Hebrew, the word for righteousness and justice is the same word. Justice brings peace - the absence of strife and conflict in every area of life - personal life, family life, social life, business life, national life, international life. Here is a simple life rule: "Trust God and do what is right (just)." Unrighteousness (Injustice) brings strife, conflict - in every area of life. Micah 6:8 states, *"What does the Lord require of thee but to do justly, to love mercy and to walk humbly (faithfully) with God."*

After Repentance -- Freshness and Joy. Chapter 35, verses 1, 6b, 7a, 10. *"The desert and the parched land will be glad; the wilderness will rejoice and blossom ... Water will gush forth in the wilderness and streams in the desert. The burning sand will become a pool, the thirsty ground bubbling springs... the ransomed of the Lord will return. They will enter Zion with singing; everlasting joy will crown their heads. Gladness and joy will overtake them, and sorrow and sighing will flee away."* This passage speaks not only to our final redemption in heaven, but also to the quality of life experienced by the person who truly repents and turns to God. There is no sweeter blessing than to recognize a sin in our lives, to confess that sin, and then, with courage and conviction, to repent of that sin -- to cast it in the fire. A young college student was convicted by the Holy Spirit, through reading the Word, that her costly collection of raunchy rock music was a sin. She started to sell the collection, but God said **no**. Then she started to give it away, but God said **no** again. Then she physically destroyed the collection, and God said **yes**. The result was that she immediately entered into a spiritual Zion with rejoicing and singing, gladness and joy overtaking her, sorrow and sighing fleeing away. Try it sometime. You will feel clean again!

God's Transparency. Chapter 45, verse 19. *"I have not spoken in secret ... I, the Lord, speak the truth; I declare what is right."* God speaks through nature and through history, but primarily, God speaks through the Bible. The Bible is the most widely translated and distributed book ever printed. God has not spoken in secret. And God speaks facts. He declares the way things really are. It is we who speak error, and attempt either through ignorance or intent, to distort the truth. Want to know what's real? Read the Word.

Standing on the Promises. Chapter 46, verse 11b. *"... what I have said, I will bring about; what I have planned, that will I do."* In Acts 27:25, Paul states, *"For I believe God, that He will do exactly what He says He will do."* This is the essence of faith. We believe that God will do exactly what He says in His Word He will do. We have a dependable, faithful God. What God promises, He will carry out. We stand on His promises.

Separation From God. Chapter 53, verse 6a; Chapter 59, verse 2a; Chapter 52, verse 11b. *"We all, like sheep, have gone astray, each of us has turned to his own way ... your iniquities have separated you from your God; ... Run! Run! Get out of there! Touch not the unclean thing! Come out from there and be pure ..."* No one can claim to be sin-free. We have all sinned and come short of the glory of God. And our sins separate us from God. Not until we recognize our sin, confess it, repent of it and receive forgiveness can we come back into fellowship with God.

Nor is anyone temptation-free. We are all tempted. But God tells us to flee from temptation. Put it out of our minds. Get away from where temptation lurks. Run from it!

Preach the Truth. Chapter 61, verse 1; Chapter 55, verse 11. *"The Spirit of the Sovereign Lord is upon me, because the Lord has anointed me to preach good news ... to proclaim freedom ... and release ... (God says) 'My word that goes out from my mouth ... will not return to me empty, but will accomplish what I desire and achieve the purpose for which I sent it.'"* We have a God who speaks. Sometimes He speaks through circumstances. Sometimes he speaks through anointed people. Always, when He speaks, it is consistent with the Bible, God's Word. God never tells us to do something which is contrary to His Word. And 'God-speak' is effective. It accomplishes what He intends it to accomplish. Maybe not in the way we want, or at the time we want. But words which come out of God's mouth make things happen -- in His way and in His time. In Genesis, we read that God literally spoke the world into existence. That is awesome.

Jeremiah

God Has a Mission for You. Chapter 1, verse 5: *"Before I formed you in the womb, I knew you; before you were born, I set you apart ..."* What a startling and energizing truth. God has known me from the beginning. The next time you start feeling sorry for yourself, remember that God has known you and loved you from the beginning. And he has 'set you apart.' Why? To be his ambassador, his hands and feet and voice, in a deceitful and wicked culture. Paul stated in Ephesians 2:10 that we are created in Christ Jesus for the purpose of doing good things for Him.

You Become Like Who or What You Worship. Chapter 2, verses 5b, 11: *"... They followed worthless idols and became worthless themselves... my people have exchanged My Glory for worthless idols."* Jeremiah is quoting 2 Kings, 17:15. We become like what we follow. If we follow Satan into sin, we become like Satan. If we follow Jesus into righteousness, we become like Jesus.

The Downhill Spiral. Chapter 2, verse 19: *"Consider then and realize how evil and bitter it is for you when you forsake the Lord your God."* Forsaking God leads downhill -- every time -- and eventually leads to hell. It may seem like freedom and fun at the beginning, but this is the deception of the Great Deceiver. Forsaking God leads to evil and eventually to sorrow, regret, frustration, confusion, bitterness, despondency, depression, and death.

No Excuse. Chapter 4, verse 18: *"Your own conduct and actions have brought this upon you."* There is no excuse. Never. We must learn to take full responsibility for our actions.

There is No Good in Evil. Chapter 5, verse 25: *"Your sins have deprived you of good."* Sin has no 'redeeming value.' Sin is the enemy of all that is good. Sin separates us from God. Repentance and turning back to God is the only solution.

What Will You Choose? Chapter 6, verse 16: *"This is what the Lord says, 'Stand at the cross roads and look; ask for the ancient paths, where the good way is, and walk in it, and you shall find rest for your souls..."* You stand at the cross roads every day. You have choices to make. If you are uncertain, ask others more experienced than yourself what they have done in similar situations. It has been said that a fool learns by his own mistakes; a wise person learns by the mistakes of others. Then you should ask yourself, "What is the good way -- the godly way." And then walk in the good way. And you will find rest for your soul.

You Can't Hide. Chapter 7, verses 2-8: *"Hear the Word of the Lord, ... 'Reform your ways and your actions and I will let you live in this place ... Will you steal, commit adultery and lie ... and then come before me in this house which bears My Name and say, 'We are safe' to do all those detestable things? ... But I have been watching,' declares the Lord."* The apostle James stated, *"Be ye doers of the word, and not hearers only ... faith without works is dead."* So what is meant by "works" in this context? Simply stated, it means a godly life characterized by purity, humility and unselfishness in thought, word and deed.

It's the Inner Man That Counts. Chapter 9, verse 25: *"The days are coming declares the Lord when I will punish all who are circumcised only in the flesh."* It is not the outward appearance which matters most to God, but rather the inner attitude and character.

Form or Substance? Chapter 12, verse 2: *"You are always on their lips, but far from their hearts."* Does this not characterize a lot of modern day Christian practice? Lots of form, but very little substance.

You Can't Escape. Chapter 12, verse 3: *"You know me, O Lord; you see me and test my thoughts about you."* The scripture states that Jesus knows what is in man's heart - his very inmost thoughts. Sobering!

Don't Starve Yourself. Chapter 15, verse 16a: *"When your words came, I ate them; they were my joy and my heart's delight..."* Jesus said, *"Man does not live by bread alone, but by every word that proceeds from the mouth of God."* The Word of God is our spiritual food. We cannot live the Christian life without a steady intake of the Word of God into our minds and hearts, any more than we can sustain physical life without a steady intake of food. Think about it. Are you starving yourself spiritually?

Are You a Student of the Word? Chapter 17, verses 7-8: *"But blessed is the man who trusts in the Lord, whose confidence is in Him. He will be like a tree planted by the water that sends out its roots by the stream. It does not fear when heat comes: its leaves are always green. It has no worries in a year of drought and never fails to bear fruit."* Jeremiah is restating the same truth stated by David in Psalm 1. Jeremiah was a student of the Word of God. All great servants of God, regardless of their status in life, are students of the Word of God.

Trust God, and Do What is Right. Chapter 17, verse 10: *"I the Lord search the heart and examine the mind to reward a man according to his conduct, according to what his deeds deserve."* Does it really matter to God what we do? Jesus said, *'By their deeds shall ye know them.'* What we do is a direct reflection of what we are inside. If our hearts are right before God, our deeds will be pleasing to Him.

He Has NOT Promised Acceptance by the World. Chapter 20, verses 8-9: *"The word of the Lord has brought me insult and reproach ... But if I say, 'I will not mention Him or speak any more in His name,' His word is in my heart like a burning fire shut up in my bones. I am weary of holding it in; indeed, I cannot.'"* We are called to be good witnesses, not to be liked and accepted. Are we good witnesses only when our words of testimony bring us appreciation and praise? Or does His Word burn in our hearts so intensely that we cannot keep silent even in the face of rejection and mockery? This is what God really wants.

What You ARE, Not What You OWN. Chapter 22, verses 14-15: *"King Jehoiakim says, 'I will build a magnificent palace with huge rooms and many windows, paneled throughout with fragrant cedar and painted a lovely red.' But (God says) a beautiful palace does not make a great king! Why did your father, Josiah, reign so long? Because he was just and right in all his dealings. That is why God blessed him"* (Living Bible). Memorize this phrase: *"A beautiful palace does not make a great king."* Apply it widely to your life. Do beautiful clothes make a godly woman? Does a sporty car make a loving husband? Do expensive golf clubs make a caring father? Does a lavish home make a gracious hostess? Rather, we should look beyond the outward appearances and seek to know the inner character of a person.

Exposed! Chapter 23, verse 24: *"'Can anyone hide in secret places so that I cannot see him,' declares the Lord?"* Noah tried, and failed. The Bible states that everything – yes, everything – is exposed and open to God. Even our private thoughts are fully known to Him. He is 'omniscient' – all knowing. The old Anglican liturgy calls for us to confess our sins of "thought, word and deed."

Ask God. Chapter 29, verse 11. *"'I know the plans I have for you,' declares the Lord, 'plans to prosper you and not to harm you, plans to give you hope and a future...'"* Think you are stuck, going nowhere? Not true. Keep reading. *"Call on me and I will answer you and tell you great and unsearchable things you do not know."* (Chapter 33, verse 3) Call on God, and He will reveal the plans He has for you, His plans to give you hope and a future.

Lamentations

Count the Cost. Chapter 1, verse 9: *"Her filthiness clung to her skirts; she did not consider her future. Her fall was astounding; there was none to comfort her."* It is a deception of Satan to blind a person to the consequences of sin. When faced with temptation, it is the smart person who considers how yielding to that temptation will affect his/her future.

The Biblical Definition of Addiction. Chapter 1, verses 14, 20: *"My sins are bound into a yoke ... around my neck ... and are choking me ... I cannot stand it... I am in torment."* This is the biblical description of addiction. How can you avoid addiction -- to alcohol, drugs, nicotine, pornography, fornication, adultery, gambling? Simply don't start. And if you have already started? Then stop -- before it becomes a rope bound around your neck, choking you, tormenting you, which it surely will. Then it is too late.

Beware of Whom You Believe. Chapter 2, verse 4. *"The visions of your prophets were false and worthless; they did not expose your sin to ward off your captivity. The oracles they gave you were false and misleading."* Just because a person is a seminary graduate and holds a pastorate or has a vast TV audience of followers does not mean that he is a trustworthy preacher of the Word. False prophets were an abomination to the Lord in biblical times. Preachers today who call evil good and good evil are likewise an abomination to the Lord. We are commanded in Scripture to be discerning and careful about whom we trust.

God Fulfills His Promises. Chapter 2, verse 17. *"The Lord has done what he planned; he has fulfilled his word."* Believing this truth is the essence of faith. God makes good on His promises. Faith is not so much believing IN God as it is simply BELIEVING God. What God says He will do, He WILL do. This is a cause for both fear and for hope. When God says that *"the wages of sin is death,"* He means it. But then when He says that *"the gift of God is eternal life through Jesus Christ,"* He means that also. One is the cause of fear, the other the cause of hope. Awesome!

New Every Morning. Chapter 3, verses 22-23. *"Because of the Lord's great love we are not consumed. For his compassions never fail. They are new every morning. Great is His faithfulness."* If we got what we deserved, we would all end up in hell. But God is a God of grace and love, as well as a God of justice, so He offers us an escape, a path through the wilderness leading to heaven. Yes, He IS faithful.

Hope in God. Chapter 3, verse 25. *"The Lord is good to those whose hope is in Him, to the one who seeks Him." Jesus said, "Seek ye FIRST the Kingdom of Heaven ..."* Am I seeking HIM – or the things He gives? There is a difference.

Vigilance Against Moral and Spiritual Decay. Chapter 4, verses 12-13a: *"The kings of the earth did not believe nor did any of the world's people, that enemies and foes could enter the gates of Jerusalem. But it happened ..."* There has not been a war on the United States mainland (with the exception of the terrorist attacks on 9-11-01) in 145 years. Enemies have not marched into Washington since the War of 1812. But that is no guarantee that the United States of America will not eventually go the way of every other great nation in history. As Patrick Henry once said, "Eternal vigilance is the price of liberty." But this does not mean vigilance against foreign threats only. It also means vigilance against the internal moral and spiritual decay which has been the common precursor of the fall of every great civilization in history.

Ezekiel

My Brother's Keeper. Chapter 2, verse 17. *"Son of man, I have made you a watchman for the house of Israel; so hear the word I speak and give them warning for me. When I say to a wicked man, 'You will surely die,' and you do NOT warn him or speak out to dissuade him from his evil ways ... that wicked man will die for his sin, and I will hold YOU accountable for his blood. But if you DO warn him and he still does not turn from his wickedness, or from his evil ways, he will die for his sin; but YOU will be saved yourself."* In chapter 33 the watchman is to give warning of the *"sword coming against the land."* When Cain was confronted by God after killing his brother Abel, Cain asked, *'Am I my brother's keeper?'* At this moment God revealed it as a biblical principle that I AM my brother's keeper. Obadiah, chapter 1, verses 10-11 states that if I stand aloof while evil rages around me, I am as guilty as those perpetrating that evil. Great civilizations have met their demise because, collectively, good citizens have stood aloof and allowed evil forces to prevail. As long as I am still living, I cannot stand aloof to the godless influences which threaten to destroy my nation, my community, my friends, my family and myself.

The Buck Stops Here. Chapter 9, verses 3-6. *"The Lord called to the man clothed in linen who had the writing kit at his side and said to him, 'Go through the city of Jerusalem and put a mark on the foreheads of those who grieve and lament at all of the detestable things that are done in Jerusalem.' As I listened he said to the others, 'Follow him through the city and kill (everyone), but do not touch anyone who has the mark on his forehead. Begin at my sanctuary.' So they began with the elders who were at the front of the temple."* Jesus stated that the teacher has the greater responsibility. Those at the highest level (those in His sanctuary) carry the greater burden and should be the first to be rooted out and disciplined for their wrongdoing. A wise general once stated, "When I give an order and it is not carried out in the manner I desired, I look first at myself, to see whether my instructions were clear, concise and complete. Next I look at my immediate subordinates to see whether they might have misconstrued or misinterpreted my instructions. And then I go on down the chain of command until I find out where and by whom my orders were misinterpreted or misapplied or disobeyed."

The Buck Stops Here - Part II. Chapter 18, verse 20. *"The soul who sins is the one who will die. The son will not share the guilt of the father, nor will the father share the guilt of the son. The righteousness of the righteous man will be credited to him and the wickedness of the wicked will be charged against him."* I alone am responsible for my actions. I cannot blame anyone else. We are currently reading about wealthy, highly placed, very visible national leaders who have been caught cheating on their taxes and are now attempting to shift the blame to their accountants. Shame on them.

Sorry, But That's the Way It Is. Chapter 18, verse 24. *"If a righteous man turns from his righteousness and commits sin ... none of the righteous things he has done will be remembered ..."* Shakespeare wrote, 'The evil that men do lives after them. The good is oft interred with their bones.' Because of Watergate, who remembers the truly great domestic and international accomplishments of President Richard Nixon? Lord, would that I might end strong!

Passing the Buck. Chapter 20, verse 4. *"Will you judge them? Will you judge them, son of man? Then confront them with their detestable practices..."* I have no right to judge the deeds of another person, either to others or in my own heart, unless I am willing to confront that person about those deeds.

The Start Point for Salvation. Chapter 20, verses 42-43. *"Then you will know that I am the Lord ... (and) you will remember your conduct and all the actions by which you have defiled yourselves ... and you will loath yourselves..."* When a person recognizes the pure and holy God for who He is, and looks at himself in comparison, then that person becomes convicted of his or her own filthiness and loathes himself. This is the beginning of salvation - to recognize the true nature of God, to stand before him naked and undone, to see your sin clearly in the light of God's holiness, to loath yourself for your sin - and then to confess that sin, repent of that sin, and turn to God.

What God Wants. Chapter 33, verse 11. *" 'As surely as I live', declares the sovereign Lord, 'I take no pleasure in the death of the wicked, but that they turn from their ways and live.' "* Jesus said that he did not come to call to repentance those who consider themselves righteous, but He came to call to repentance those who recognize, admit and confess their utter sinfulness and wretchedness before a Holy God. Why not those in the first category? Because in their arrogant self-righteousness they admit no sin and therefore would never respond to a message of repentance. Such a message is offensive to them. But God takes no pleasure in the death of the wicked. Indeed, He would that every man confess their sins and turn to Him for life eternal. But there is no salvation without the recognition of sin. "Amazing grace, how sweet the sound, that saved a wretch like me."

Ugh! Does This Describe Me? Chapter 33, verses 31-32. *"My people come to you, as they usually do, to sit before you to listen to your words, but they do not put them into practice. With their mouths they express devotion, but their hearts (are exceedingly selfish). Indeed, to them, you are nothing more than one who sings love songs with a beautiful voice and plays an instrument well, for they hear your words but do not put them into practice."* James said, *"Be ye doers of the word, and not hearers only."* The proof of faith is a life lived in obedience to the Word of God.

The Ultimate Purpose of Leadership. Chapter 34, verses 2, 4, 8. *"Woe to those leaders ... who only take care of themselves. Should not the leader take care of his followers? ... You have not strengthened the weak or taken care of the sick, or bound up the injured. You have not brought back the strays or searched for the lost ... I (the Lord) hold leaders responsible for their followers ..."* Do you aspire to leadership? For what purpose? The only legitimate purpose is to serve those who would be your followers.

A Promise of God to Leaders. Chapter 44, verse 15 - 16. *"The (leaders) who faithfully carry out their duties ... They alone are to enter my sanctuary."* Is God interested in your faithfulness and competence as a leader? Read the verse again for the answer.

Are You A Fresh Water Person? Chapter 47, verses 7-10, 22-23. *"Then (the Lord) led me back to the bank of the river. When I arrived there, I saw a great number of trees on each side of the river. He said to me, 'This water flows ... down through the Jordan valley, and enters the Dead Sea. Where it empties into the sea, the water there becomes fresh. Swarms of living creatures will live wherever the river flows. There will be large numbers of fish, because this (fresh) water flows there and makes the salt water fresh; so where the river flows, everything will live.'"* If you are truly living for the Lord Jesus Christ, you will be like the fresh water spoken of above. Everywhere you go you will generate joy, and hope, and truth, and faith, and peace and purpose in the lives of those you touch. All of us who are Christians are to be influencers of the people and culture around us - turning the salt water into fresh water so that the life of God can spring up and flourish in the lives of others.

Daniel

A Profile in Courage.

Daniel is the last of the major prophets. Although his prophesies of the end times are significant, it is his character which gives us a model for our own lives. He is one of the prime Biblical examples of personal and professional excellence.

Self-discipline. Daniel 1:1-8. *"But Daniel resolved not to defile himself with royal food and wine."*

Wisdom and understanding. Daniel 1:20. *"In every matter of wisdom and understanding about which the king questioned (Daniel), the king found (Daniel) ten times better than (anyone else in) the whole kingdom."*

Tactful. Daniel 2:14. *"Daniel spoke to him (the commander of the king's guard) with wisdom and tact."*

Faithfulness to God. Daniel 2:27 *"Daniel replied (to the king) ... 'there is a God in heaven who reveals mysteries.'"*

Humility. Daniel 2:30. (Daniel is speaking to the king.) *"...this mystery has been revealed to me, not because I have greater wisdom than other men, but so that you, O King, may know the interpretation and that you may understand ..."*

Loyal to his friends. Daniel 2:49. *"At Daniel's request, the king appointed Shadrach, Meshach and Abednego administrators over the entire province of Babylon ..."*

Courage to Confront. Daniel 5:25-30. (Daniel is speaking to the king.) *"But you did not honor the God who holds in his hand your life and all your ways."*

Positive Outlook. Daniel 6:3. *"But Daniel was preferred above the presidents and princes because an excellent spirit was in him ..."*

Professionally Competent. Daniel 6:3. *"Daniel distinguished himself among the administrators ... by his exceptional qualities (of leadership)."*

Trustworthy, Incorruptible, Diligent. Daniel 6:4-5. *"He was trustworthy and neither corrupt nor negligent."*

Integrity. Daniel 6:10. *"Now when Daniel learned of the decree (forbidding anyone to pray to any God for 30 days) he went home to the upstairs room where the windows opened toward Jerusalem. Three times a day he got down on his knees and prayed, giving thanks to his God, JUST AS HE HAD DONE BEFORE..."*

Respect for Authority. Daniel 6:21. *"Daniel answered, 'O King, live forever...'"*

His Reward. Daniel 6:28. *"So Daniel prospered during the reign of Darius and the reign of Cyrus the Persian."*

The Minor Prophets

Hosea

Hosea is the first of the 12 "Minor Prophets". They are called "minor" not that they are of any less importance than the "major" prophets but simply because their writings are shorter than those of the "major" prophets.

The Book of Hosea is about Israel's unfaithfulness to God, the penalties for that unfaithfulness, and God's faithfulness to Israel despite Israel's unfaithfulness to God.

Israel's unfaithfulness is likened to adultery. It is not a pretty picture.

The Nation is Guilty. Chapter 1, verse 2b: *"... the land (*Israel*) is guilty of the vilest adultery in departing from the Lord."* This sets the stage for the remainder of the book.

No Acknowledgment of God. Chapter 4, verses 1-3*: "There is no faithfulness, no love, no acknowledgment of God in the land. There is only cursing, lying and murder, stealing and adultery, they break all bounds and bloodshed follows bloodshed. Because of this the land mourns, and all who live in it waste away."* The key here is *"... no acknowledgment of God in the land."* This is a powerful and constant lesson of history. When a nation (i.e., the people of the land) abandon God, the very foundation for peace, security and prosperity crumbles.

Rejecting the Truth. Chapter 4, verses 6, 7, 10, 11, 14: *"They have rejected knowledge... ignored the law of God... exchanged my glory for something disgraceful... deserted the law... to give themselves to prostitution... a people without understanding will come to ruin."* The Apostle Paul stated, *"For I believe God, that it will happen just as He has stated."*

When They Admit Their Guilt. Chapter 5, verses 14-15*: "... when they admit their guilt; they will seek my face; in their misery they will earnestly (return to) me."* Jesus used this same theme in his parable of the prodigal son.

God Desires a Changed Heart. Chapter 6, verse 6: *"For I desire mercy, not sacrifice, and acknowledgment of God rather than burnt offerings."* God is not interested in FORMS of worship. What He wants is SUBSTANCE in worship.

But They Became Vile. Chapter 9, verse 10: *"They dedicated themselves to that shameful (practice) and became as vile as the thing they loved."* We somehow morph into the likeness of that which we worship and love, be it good or evil. A biblical principle.

We Reap What We Sow. Chapter 8, verse 7; chapter 10, verse 12: *"They sow the wind (unfaithfulness) and reap the whirlwind (destruction)... Sow for yourselves righteousness and reap the fruit of unfailing love."* We reap what we sow.

God Is Faithful. Chapter 11, verses 4, 8: *"I led them with cords of human kindness, with ties of love... My heart is changed within me; all my compassion is aroused."* God cannot deny his essential nature.

Who Is Really Wise. Chapter 14, verse 9: *"Who is wise? He will realize these things. Who is discerning? He will understand them. The ways of the Lord are right; the righteous walk in them, but the rebellious stumble in them."* God gives us freedom to choose His ways or disregard His ways. He longs for us to walk in His ways, just as a father longs for his son to follow the father's advice. It breaks God's heart when we rebel. But He allows us to do so. And He welcomes us back into His arms when we confess, repent and return to Him.

Joel

The book of Joel is the story of national economic collapse, a call by the prophet Joel to confession and repentance, the turning back of the people of Israel to God, and the full restoration of national prosperity.

By implication, on the personal, individual level, Joel is also a story of moral degradation and disaster, and a call to personal repentance, confession and turning back to God, followed by God's full forgiveness and restoration.

Economic Collapse. Chapter 1, verse 12. *"The harvest of the field is destroyed, the vine is dried up and the fig tree is withered; the pomegranate, and the apple tree - all the trees of the field are dried up. Surely the joy of the people is withered away."* The foundation of the economy of Israel was agriculture; and a devastating, sustained plague of locusts had destroyed the crops completely. As the crops were destroyed, so also the joy of the people withered away. Joel calls the plague of locusts the judgment of God because of the sins of the nation. Sin, both on the national and personal levels, always brings devastation, destruction, and misery, to some degree. ALWAYS - maybe not immediately -- but ALWAYS.

The Beginning of the Recovery. Chapter 1, verse 14. *"Declare a holy fast, call a sacred assembly. Summon the elders and all who live in the land to the house of the Lord your God, and cry out to the Lord."* The Prophet Joel says don't just sit there wallowing in your misery, do something! Specifically, call a meeting of the elders and the people and cry out to God.

Returning to the Lord. Chapter 2, verse 13. *"Rend your heart and not your garments. Return to the Lord your God, for He is gracious and compassionate, slow to anger and abounding in love, and he relents from sending calamity."* Get serious about your sins, Joel says. Tear your hearts, not your garments. In confession and repentance, God wants substance, not form. God is a God of what is real. He cannot be fooled by superficiality. When a person really means business with God, that person finds that God is responsive, gracious and compassionate.

God's Response. Chapter 2, verse 28. *"And afterward, I will pour out my Spirit on all people. Your sons and daughters will prophesy, your old men will dream dreams, your young men will see visions. Even on my servants, both men and women, I will pour out my spirit in those days."* The result of true repentance by a nation is a pouring out of God's spirit on ALL of the people. There will be an evident change in the people and the way they live.

Spiritual and Economic Recovery. Chapter 3, verse 18. *"In that day the mountains will drip new wine, and the hills will flow with milk; all of the ravines of Judah will run with water. A fountain will flow out of the Lord's house and will water the (entire) valley."* After national confession and repentance comes economic restoration. The crisis ends. Prosperity comes again. But it doesn't come from the wisdom of godless economists. It comes from the justice and compassion of God. The prophet Isaiah also proclaimed this restoration when he stated (Isaiah 35:6, verse 1), *"Water will gush forth in the wilderness and streams in the desert. The burning sand will become a pool, the thirsty ground bubbling springs... the wilderness will rejoice and blossom..."* Where are you personally, at this moment of your life? Is your life a story of moral degradation and disaster, barrenness and burning sand? There IS hope, but not from anything this world can offer. True hope is in God, in His graciousness and compassion. Through honest confession and genuine repentance, there is hope, there is restoration.*" A fountain will flow out of the Lord's house and water the whole desolate valley* (of your life)*... It will blossom, ... and (*you*) will rejoice."* This is the promise of God as proclaimed by the Prophet Joel.

Amos

In *"The Message,"* author Eugene H. Peterson states the following in his introduction to the book of Amos;

> "More people are exploited and abused in the cause of religion than in any other way... The moment a person (or government, or religion or organization) is convinced that God is either ordering or sanctioning a cause or project, anything goes. The history, worldwide, of religious fueled hate, killing, and oppression is staggering. ... The biblical prophets continue to be the most powerful and effective voices ever heard on this earth for keeping religion honest, humble and compassionate. Prophets sniff out injustice, especially injustice that is dressed up in religious garb... Prophets see through hypocrisy, especially hypocrisy that assumes a religious pose. Prophets are not impressed by position or power or authority. They aren't taken in by numbers, size or appearances of success... A spiritual life that doesn't give a large place to prophet-articulated justice will end up making us worse instead of better, separating us from God's ways instead of drawing us into them."

Chapter 1 of Amos, plus the first 5 verses of chapter 2, are an indictment of the sinful ways of Israel's neighbors - Syria, Gaza, Tyre, Edom, Jordan, Moab and Judah. The remainder of Amos addresses the hypocrisy and evils of the leaders, priests and people of Israel, and God's judgment on their sins. There is an alarming parallel in world cultures today.

Rebellion Against the Lord. Chapter 2, verses 11-13. *"I raised up prophets among your sons, and Nazirites among your young men. Is this not true, you people of Israel? But you made the Nazirites drink wine and commanded the prophets not to prophesy. Because of this I will crush you..."* God raised up prophets to proclaim the truth and to keep the people aware of the encroachment of evil influences. God also raised up Nazirites to set an example of Godly living. The Nazirites made a vow to abstain from drinking alcoholic wine. But the Israelite society as a whole had become self-indulgent, arrogant and corrupt. They scoffed at the Law of the Lord, practicing the forms of religion but denying its real substance - justice, mercy and faithfulness. And not only did they force the Nazirites to break their vows and drink wine, but they commanded the prophets to shut up. Today, in America, the powerful abortion lobby is preparing legislation which would force Christian doctors to perform abortions or lose their licenses.

And the powerful homosexual lobby is preparing legislation which would make preaching the biblical view of homosexuality a criminal offense. Will God also crush America for these offenses, just as he crushed the Israelites and sent them into exile for 70 years?

Complacency. Chapter 6, verse 1. *"Woe to you who are complacent in Zion..."* In the Holocaust Museum in Washington, there is displayed a quotation by German pastor Martin Niemoller: "In Germany, they (the Nazis) first came for the Communists, but I didn't speak up because I wasn't a Communist. Then they came for the Jews, but I didn't speak up because I wasn't a Jew. Then they came for the Trade Unionists, but I didn't speak up because I wasn't a Trade Unionist. Then they came for the Catholics, but I was a Protestant so I didn't speak up. And then they came for me, and by that time there was no one left to speak up." Do we not realize that in our own country the Satanic forces of evil are virulent and cunning and always on the offensive? The Apostle Peter stated, *"Be sober, be vigilant, because your adversary the devil, as a roaring lion, walketh about seeking whom he may devour."* Edmund Burke (1729-1797) stated, "The only thing necessary for the triumph of evil is for good men to do nothing."

Justice. Chapter 5, verses 7, 10, 12, 21-24. *"You turn justice into bitterness and cast righteousness to the ground... you hate the one who testifies in court and despise him who tells the truth... you take bribes and subvert justice (and yet you continue to practice the outward forms of religion)... I hate, I despise your religious feasts, I cannot stand your assemblies. Even though you bring me burnt offerings I will not accept them... Away with the noise of your songs. I will not listen to the music of your harps. Rather, let justice roll like a river and righteousness like a never failing stream."* There is no theme in the writings of all of the prophets more compelling than justice - doing what is right before God and treating others fairly, out of a pure heart and a clear conscience. Jesus confirms this as one of the three principles of holy living. In Matthew 23:23, speaking to the hypocritical Pharisees, Jesus proclaims, *"You have neglected the weightier matters of the law - justice, mercy and faithfulness."*

Obadiah

The Result of Pride. Chapter 1, verses 3-4. *"The pride of your heart has deceived you ... you who say to yourself, 'Who can bring me down to the ground?' Though you soar like the eagle and make your nest among the stars, from there I will bring you down,' declares the Lord."* Webster defines pride as inordinate self-esteem, conceit, vanity, vainglory, arrogance. In the biblical sense, pride is a spirit of defiance, rebellion, of independence from God, the belief that God is irrelevant to your life. Humility, on the other hand, is the spirit of submission to God, the wisdom that without God, you are helpless, lost. Observe the contrast in excerpts from these two famous poems. In *Invictus*, William Ernest Henley writes, "I am the master of my fate, I am the captain of your soul." In *The Recessional*, Rudyard Kipling writes, "Still stands Thine ancient sacrifice, a humble and a contrite heart." In Daniel 4:7, Nebuchadnezzar states, *"Those who walk in pride, God is able to bring down."*

It is a Sin to do Nothing to Prevent Evil. Chapter 1, verses 10-12: *"Because of the violence against your brother Jacob, you will be covered with shame, you will be destroyed forever. On the day you stood aloof while strangers carried off his wealth and foreigners entered his gates and cast lots for Jerusalem, you (Edom) were like one of them. You should not look down on your brother in the day of his misfortune."* It is a sin to do nothing to prevent an evil from happening to a friend. Think about it. Am I standing aloof while some injustice is being perpetrated against my friend? Is it morally right to take up arms to defend the weak and defenseless? Augustine thought so.

What You Do Unto Others Will Be Done Unto You. Chapter 1, verse 15b: *"As you have done, it will be done to you; your deeds will return upon your own head."* This is a sobering biblical truth. The way I am treating others, either for good or for evil, is surely the way I will also eventually be treated.

Jonah

The trouble with Jonah is that he had a bad attitude. He believed in God, he heard the voice of God, he was a discerning theologian, he was a faithful witness, he had integrity, he was a man of prayer, he was an extremely effective preacher -- but he had a bad attitude.

Jonah's Disobedience. Chapter 1, verses 1-3. *"The Word of the Lord came to Jonah, son of Amittai: 'Go to the great city of Nineveh and preach against it, because its wickedness has come up before me.' But Jonah ran away from the Lord and headed to Tarshish."* Jonah had a bad attitude toward Nineveh. According to his own statement in chapter 4, the reason he disobeyed God and headed for Tarshish was that he knew that if he went to Nineveh and preached, the people would repent and turn to God, and Jonah didn't want this to happen. Are there non-Christians who have slandered us or hurt our careers that we would just as soon never hear about Jesus and receive the grace of God?

Jonah's Bold and Honest Witness. Chapter 1, verses 4-16. *"All the sailors were afraid and each cried out to his own god... Jonah said, 'I am a Hebrew and I worship the Lord, the God of heaven who made the sea and the land.' ... This terrified them, so they asked him, 'What should we do to make the sea calm down for us?'... Jonah said, 'Pick me up and throw me into the sea so it will become calm. I know that it is my fault that this great storm has come upon you.' ... Instead, the men did their best to row back to land, but they could not... Then they cried to the Lord, 'O Lord, please do not let us die for taking this man's life'... Then they threw Jonah overboard and the raging sea grew calm. At this the men greatly feared the Lord and offered sacrifices to the Lord and made vows to Him."* An amazing account. At first, each of the men cried out to his own god. Then Jonah witnessed to them about the true God. They were terrified. They turned to Jonah to find out what to do. He told them. Jonah took responsibility for his own actions - a basic element of integrity. After another effort at rowing to shore, they did as Jonah had stated and threw him overboard. The seas grew calm and the men feared and worshipped the Lord. *("The fear of the Lord is the beginning of wisdom.")* The men went from crying out to their own Gods to fearing and worshiping the true God because of Jonah's faithful witness and demonstrated integrity.

Forfeiting God's Grace. Chapter 2, verse 1. *"From inside the fish, Jonah prayed to the Lord his God."* Except for the first and last verses, all of chapter 2 is Jonah's prayer. Tucked away in his prayer is a statement of remarkable insight. (Verse 8) *"Those who cling to worthless idols forfeit the grace that could be theirs."* Whatever the idol (career, money, power, ambition, sex, alcohol, drugs), it stands in the way of the wonderful, freeing, life giving grace of God. It's the classic case of, 'You simply don't know what you are missing.'

God Answers Prayer. Chapter 2, verse 10. *"And the Lord commanded the fish, and it vomited Jonah onto dry land."* God hears and answers the genuine prayers of a truly repentant person.

Jonah Obeys. Chapter 3, verses 1-3. *"The word of the Lord came to Jonah a second time: 'Go to Nineveh and proclaim the message I give you.' Jonah obeyed the word of the Lord and went to Nineveh."* God does give us all second chances. He is a loving and compassionate God.

Jonah Speaks. Chapter 3, verses 4-5. *"Jonah proclaimed as God had directed him, 'Forty more days and Nineveh will be destroyed.' The Ninevites believed God."* When a preacher preaches what God commands him to preach, people are converted.

God's Response. Chapter 3, verse 10; Chapter 4, verse 1. *"When God saw... how they turned from their evil ways, he had compassion on them and did not bring on them the destruction he had threatened. But Jonah was greatly displeased and became angry."* In childish petulance, Jonah complains that God has made a fool of him before the people of Nineveh by not bringing down the destruction Jonah had threatened. But God does not command us to be His witnesses so that WE will look good. He commands us to be His witnesses so the HE will look good.

Jonah's Limited Vision. Chapter 4, verse 10. *"But the Lord said, you have been concerned about this vine... But I was concerned about that great city."* We often get ensnared in selfish, petty details. God's purposes are much bigger.

Micah

The Downward Spiral. Chapter 2, verse 2; Chapter 3, verse 1; Chapter 7 verse 7. *"They covet fields and seize them. They defraud a man of his home, a fellow man of his inheritance...Should you not know justice, you who hate good and love evil...The judge accepts bribes, the powerful dictate what they desire - they all conspire together."* Sound familiar? The only constant, the only thing on earth which has never changed and never will change, is human nature. We are all infected with a sinful nature, and we are all subject to the corruption of spirit. But there is good news. In Romans 7:24, Paul states; *"Who will rescue me from this body of death? Thanks be to God - through Jesus Christ our Lord."* We cannot do it alone. Only through our relationship with Jesus Christ and our obedience to His Word can we escape *"the corruption which is in the world through our sinful desires."* 2 Peter 1:4

The Cesspool of Corruption. Chapter 3, verse 11. *"Her leaders judge for a bribe, her priests teach for a price, and her prophets tell fortunes for money."* Bribe - Price - Money. 1 Peter 6:10 teaches, *"For the love of money is the root of all evil..."* Corruption. The love of money. We were visiting a European country and I had been given an appointment with the Attorney General of that country. He was a Christian. I asked him, "What is the greatest problem you face." And his immediate reply was, "Corruption." He had recently put a member of the President's cabinet in prison for fraud and the head of his own political party was under investigation for accepting bribes. And it is not just in the offices of government. Look around you, in your church, in the parachurch ministry you support. What is the primary emphasis? Is it soul winning? - or fund raising? Look into your own soul. Are you compromising the basics of your faith to possess the toys which only money can buy?

God's Will for You - and Me. Chapter 6, verse 8. *"He has shown you, oh man, what is good. And what does the Lord require of you? To act justly, to love mercy, and to walk humbly with your God."* Compare this to Jesus' charge to the Pharisees in Matthew 23:23. *"But you have neglected the more important matters of the law -- justice, mercy, faithfulness."* Justice. Mercy. Faithfulness. Want to know how God wants you to live? You don't have to look any further. He wants you to be a person of justice, mercy and faithfulness. Justice: doing what is right and fair and just. Mercy: doing what is compassionate and considerate of others. Faithfulness: In humility, being faithful to God, to your wife and family, to your friends, to your country, to your profession. This is how God wants you to live.

Nahum

Nahum is the second of the books of the minor prophets which features the city of Nineveh. The book of Jonah told of God's concern for this "great city." The book of Nahum reveals God's anger at Nineveh for enslaving His people, and for Nineveh's shameless sinfulness. Although hundreds of miles from Jerusalem, near what is now the city of Mosul in northern Iraq, Nineveh's evil influence was great and widespread. God does not countenance sin anywhere at any time. Sin has no "redeeming value."

The Lord is Just. Chapter 1, verse 3: *"The Lord is slow to anger and great in power. He will not leave the guilty unpunished."* It is a fact of life that God is a God of justice and is in control. No one who is guilty will go unpunished. Only the fear of the Lord can make this fact come alive and cause us to confess and repent. *"The fear of the Lord is the beginning of wisdom."*

The Lord is Good. Chapter 1, verse 7: *"The Lord is good, a refuge in times of trouble. He cares for those who trust in Him."* This verse, which comes early in the book of Nahum, sets the stage for the remainder of the book. Nineveh has enslaved God's people. But God is their refuge. He cares for them. He will now take vengeance on Nineveh.

The Lord is the Avenger. Chapter 2, verses 1-2: *"An attacker advances against you, Nineveh. Guard the fortress, watch the road, brace yourselves, marshal all your strength. The Lord will restore all the splendor of Jacob, like the splendor of Israel, although destroyers have laid them waste and have ruined their vines."* Brace yourself, Nineveh. God is about to strike.

Sin Has No Redeeming Value. Chapter 3, verses 3-5: *"(There will be) many casualties, piles of dead, bodies without number, people stumbling over the corpses, all because of your wanton lust which enslaved nations and peoples ... 'I am against you', declares the Lord, 'I will lift your skirts over your faces and show the nations your nakedness.'"* Not only is God going to destroy Nineveh, He is going to embarrass Nineveh in front of the whole world, make an example of her.

"Thus Always to Tyrants." Chapter 3, verse 19: *"Everyone who hears the news about you claps his hands at your fall..."* This is the ultimate fate of tyrants. Their fall is cheered all around the world.

Habakkuk

An Age Old Quandary. Chapter 1, verse 3: *"Why do You make me look at injustice? Why do You tolerate wrong? Destruction and violence are before me; there is strife, and conflict abounds. Therefore the law is paralyzed, and justice never prevails. The wicked hem in the righteous, so that justice is perverted."* The book begins with Habakkuk frustrated and perplexed that God seemingly often allows evil to go unpunished in the world. It is an age old quandary with which all thinking persons wrestle. The book ends with one of the strongest statements of faith in the entire Bible. (See last entry in Habakkuk, below).

The Central Cry of the Reformation. Chapter 2, verse 4: *"The righteous will live by his faith."* The truth proclaimed in this verse spawned and fired the Protestant Reformation. Martin Luther proclaimed, "The just shall live by faith - alone." The cry of the Reformation was "Sola Fide" - by faith alone. And so it was from the beginning. (Genesis 15:6) *"Abram believed God, and it was credited to him as righteousness."* -- (John 5:24). *"I tell you the truth, whoever hears my word and believes on Him who sent me, has eternal life and will not be condemned; he has crossed over from death to life."* -- (Romans 1:17) *"For in the gospel a righteousness from God is revealed, a righteousness that is by faith from first to last, just as it is written: 'The just shall live by faith.'"* -- (Romans 5:1) *"Therefore since we have been justified by faith, we have peace with God through our Lord Jesus Christ, through whom we have gained access by faith into this grace in which we now stand."* -- (Ephesians 2:8-9) *"For it is by grace that you have been saved, through faith - and this not from yourselves, it is the gift of God, not by works, so that no one can boast."*

Looking For Hope in the Wrong Places. Chapter 2, verses 19-20. *"Woe to him who says to wood, 'Come to life!' or to a lifeless stone, 'Wake up.' Can it give you guidance? It is covered with gold and silver, but there is no breath in it. But the Lord is in His holy temple. Let all the earth be silent* (stand in reverent awe) *before Him."* Every human attempt to find hope and fulfillment in material possessions is doomed to failure. God - and ONLY God - is the answer to our deepest longings and our only hope for life eternal.

Stripped Down, Unadulterated Faith. Chapter 3, verses 17-18. *"Though the fig tree does not bud and there are no grapes on the vines, though the olive crop fails and the fields produce no food, though there are no sheep in the pen and no cattle in the stalls, yet I will rejoice in the Lord, I will be joyful in God my Savior."* This is one of the most powerful statements of faith in all of the Bible. Our sufficiency is of God alone. Our identity is with God alone. Our hope is from God alone. Our life is in God alone. Nothing else. No one else. And it is by faith alone. "Sola fide."

Zephaniah

He Is the Same - Yesterday, Today and Forever. Chapter 3, verses 1-4. *"Woe to the city (nation) of oppressors, rebellious and defiled! She obeys no one, she accepts no correction. She does not trust the Lord, she does not draw near to her God. Her officials are roaring lions, her rulers are ravening wolves ... Her prophets are arrogant; they are treacherous men. Her priests profane the sanctuary and do violence to the law. (BUT) the Lord within her is righteous; he does no wrong. Morning by morning he dispenses justice, and every new day he does not fail."* Regardless of how vile our nation, our people, our political leaders and our religious leaders may become, God does not change. He is a God of justice, mercy and faithfulness. We can count on Him. We can trust Him. We can rest in Him.

After John 3:16, One of the Most Important Verses in the Bible. Chapter 3, verse 17. *"The Lord your God is with you. He is mighty to save. He takes great delight in you. He comforts you with his love. He rejoices over you with singing."*

This is an encouraging and beautiful five-part statement of how God relates to you. And it is a model of how fathers and mothers should relate to their children.

1. Fathers and mothers, you should be *'with'* your children. As often as possible. Physically, intellectually, morally, spiritually. At every stage of their growing up years.

2. You should *'save'* them - protect them from every evil influence which would damage them physically, intellectually, morally, spiritually, as they are growing up.

3. You should *'take great delight'* in them - in every activity of their lives. Really enjoy them. Delight in them. Affirm them. Listen to them. Appreciate them. Love them. Bless them.

4. You should *'quiet'* them with your love. When they go through their normal (yes, extreme) ups and downs, you should be their steadying influence. Calm them with your presence and love.

5. And you should *'rejoice over them with singing.'* Actually sing to them. Whether you have a good voice or not. Take them up in your arms and dance around the room, singing to them. Do it often. Even your teenagers!

Fathers and Mothers, God is and does all these five things with you. You should also do them with your children. It will change their lives. And it will change yours.

Haggai

The basic message of the book of Haggai is the same as the message of Jesus, *"Seek ye first the Kingdom of God and His righteousness and all these things will be added unto you."* (Matthew 6:33)

The remnant of the people who remained in Palestine during the 70 year exile to Persia had allowed the temple to fall into ruin even while the people were living in fine houses. As a result, God caused an economic recession. Then God spoke through the prophet Haggai to the governor of Judah and the son of the high priest, inspiring them to rebuild the temple. As the work got started, God once again blessed the people with abundance.

Five times in Haggai God tells the people to *"give careful thought"* to the correlation between their relationship to Him and their economic wellbeing. There is a message here for us today.

The final statement in Haggai is a thrilling confirmation concerning how God blesses a leader who honors God by obeying Him.

Give Careful Thought. Chapter 1, verses 1, 4-7, 9 -10. *"The word of the Lord came through the prophet Haggai to Zerubbabel... governor of Judah, and to Joshua, son of... the high priest... 'Is this a time for you yourselves to be living in your paneled houses, while (my) house remains a ruin?... Give careful thought to your ways. You have planted much but harvested little...Give careful thought to your ways... you expected much, but see, it turned out to be little... Why? ... Because of my house, which remains a ruin, while each of you is busy with his own house. Therefore because of you the heavens have withheld their dew and the earth its crops.'"*

After Careful Thought, the Light Dawns. Chapter 1, verses 12-14. *"Then Zerubbabel...Joshua... and the whole remnant of the people obeyed the voice of the Lord their God... And the people feared the Lord... So the Lord stirred up the heart of Zerubbabel...Joshua... and the whole remnant of the people. They came and began to work on the house of the Lord..."* They obeyed by giving careful thought to their ways. Then they realized that what God had said about the cause of their economic decline was true. This caused them to fear the Lord. With their attitudes now right, their spirits were able to be stirred up by the Lord and they went to work rebuilding the house of the Lord.

Strengthened by His Spirit. Chapter 2, verses 1-7. *"The word of the Lord came through the prophet Haggai to Zerubbabel... and to Joshua... and to the remnant of the people. 'Be strong, O Zerubbabel... Be strong, O Joshua...Be strong, all you people of the land...and work. For I am with you... and my spirit remains among you. Do not fear."* When God calls us to perform a long and difficult task in His name, he does not abandon us when the process becomes tedious and backbreaking. He is there, all the time, to encourage and strengthen us by His spirit. But we must listen for His voice.

God Acts on the Basis of Our Sincerity. Chapter 2, verses 15, 18-19. *"Give careful thought to this from this day on -- consider how things were before one stone was laid on another...give careful thought to the day when the foundation of the Lord's temple was laid...Give careful thought (because) ... from this day on I will bless you."* When God saw that the people were serious in their dedication to the task of rebuilding His temple, he began to restore their prosperity.

God Blesses the Totally Dedicated Leader. Chapter 2, verse 23. *"...'I will take you, my servant Zerubbabel...' declares the Lord, 'And I will make you like my signet ring, for I have chosen you (for my special blessing).'"* Zerubbabel, the governor of Judah, responded wholeheartedly to God's tasking and rebuilt the temple. When God finds a leader who is totally dedicated to the accomplishment of tasks He has given to be done, He pours out His blessings on that leader and that people.

"Seek ye first the Kingdom of God and His righteousness and all these things will be added unto you" (Matthew 6:33).

Zechariah

Essentially, Zechariah is a call to return to God and the blessings of so doing. It is a consistent major theme throughout both the Old and New Testaments.

Return and Repent. Chapter 1, verse 2: *"'Return to me,' declares the Lord Almighty, 'and I will return to you.'"* The first teaching of John the Baptist was, *'Repent, for the Kingdom of God is at hand.'* The first teaching of Jesus was, *'Repent, for the Kingdom of God is at hand.'* Everything good in life begins with repentance - returning to God.

God Plays by the Rules - His Rules. Chapter 1, verse 6: *"Then they repented and said, 'The Lord God Almighty has done to us what our ways and practices deserve...'"* Jeremiah 4:18 states, *"Your own conduct and actions have brought this upon you."* An essential part of repentance is the recognition that sin has consequences. Repentance is an admission of guilt, a confession of sin, and a soul deep desire to change. Only then can there be forgiveness and restoration.

Repentance Brings Joy. Chapter 2, verse 4: *"'Jerusalem will be a city without walls... I myself will be a wall around it,' declares the Lord, 'And I will be its glory within.'"* Chapter 8, verse 4: *"Once again men and women of ripe old age will sit in the streets of Jerusalem... the city streets will be filled with boys and girls playing there."* This is the result of repentance, of returning to God. He then 'returns to us' and fills life with gladness and joy.

Again - Justice, Mercy and Faithfulness. Chapter 7, verses 9-10: *"This is what the Lord Almighty says: 'Administer justice; show mercy and compassion to one another. Do not oppress the widow or the fatherless, the alien or the poor. In your hearts, do not think evil of each other.'"* This is the fruit we are to produce - *"in keeping with repentance,"* as John the Baptist taught in Matthew 3:8. Before repentance comes, first, the recognition of sin, and second, confession. After repentance comes forgiveness and restoration of an unfettered relationship with God. And then comes action - a life characterized by *justice, mercy and faithfulness.* (Micah 6:8)

But By My Spirit. Chapter 4, verse 6: *"'Not by might, nor by power, but by my Spirit,' says the Lord."* Nothing worthwhile in God's sight is achieved by human strength alone. It is God's Spirit, using His Word (the 'sword of the Spirit'), that reveals sin and gives us the desire to confess and repent. Then it is God who forgives and restores. And it is by God's Spirit, again using His Word as His sword, that we are enabled to live a life characterized by justice, mercy and faithfulness.

Malachi

Malachi says, "Remain Faithful."

Cutting Corners. Chapter 1, verses 8-14: *"'When you bring blind animals for sacrifice, is that not wrong? When you sacrifice crippled or diseased animals, is that not wrong? Try offering them to your governor! Would he be pleased with you?' says the Lord Almighty... 'Cursed is the cheat who has an acceptable male in his flock and vows to give it, but then sacrifices a blemished animal to the Lord...'"* The point here is that God is not satisfied with our leftovers. He wants our best. He KNOWS that anything less will cause us gradually to waste away into irrelevance because we have put other gods before Him.

Breaking Faith with your Wife. Chapter 2, verses 13-15: *"Another thing you do. You flood the Lord's altar with your tears. You weep and wail because He no longer pays attention to your offerings or accepts them with pleasure from your hands. You ask 'Why?' It is because the Lord is acting as witness between you and the wife of your youth, because you have broken faith with her though she is your partner, the wife of your marriage covenant. Has not the Lord made them (husband and wife) one? In flesh and spirit they are His... So guard yourself in your spirit and do not break faith with the wife of your youth."* There are so many ways of breaking faith, and having a physical sexual affair isn't the only way. Here are just a few ways of breaking faith with your wife (or husband): inattention, neglect, disrespect, lack of love, lack of affection, physical or emotional abuse, sexual unfaithfulness -- either mental (pornography) or physical (sexual involvement of any kind with another person). Do you feel that your prayers are not getting through to God? Check your relationship with your spouse. Maybe that is the reason. It is a precious and wonderful thing to be at one with each other - both in the flesh and in the spirit.

Divorce? Chapter 3, verse 16: *"'I hate divorce', says the Lord God of Israel..."* It can't be made any more clear than this. God does not condone divorce. He hates it. Yes, it happens, even among Christians, but this is not the way God planned it or wants it. Marriage is a three way covenant - husband, wife and God. Break the covenant, and you get broken.

The Consequences of Evil and Good. Chapter 4, verses 1-2: *"'Surely the day is coming; it will burn like a furnace. All the arrogant and every evildoer will be stubble, and that day that is coming will set them on fire,' says the Lord Almighty.*

'Not a root or a branch will be left. But for you who revere my name, the Son of righteousness will rise with healing in His wings. And you will go out and leap like calves released from the stall.'" Grace is not cheap. God punishes the evil and rewards those who revere His name.

Love God, Love One Another - This is His Command. Chapter 4, verse 4. *"Remember (obey) the law of My servant Moses, the decrees and laws I gave him... for all Israel."* In the final analysis, it all comes down to obedience. Jesus said, *"Whoever has my commandments and obeys them, he is the one who loves me. He who loves me will be loved by my Father, and I too will love Him and show myself to him... This is my command, 'Love each other.'"* (John 14:21, 15:17) This is not legalism. It is the way of God. Obeying God sums up the whole teaching of the Old Testament - and also the New Testament. When asked what is the greatest commandment? Jesus said: *"'Love the Lord your God with all your heart and with all your soul and with all your mind.' This is the first and greatest commandment. And the second is like it, 'Love your neighbor as yourself.' All of the Law and the teaching of the Prophets are summarized in these two commandments."* (Matthew 22:37-40.) These are the commands to be obeyed. Love God. Love one another.

A Final Note

When Jesus and the writers of the New Testament refer to the 'Word of God' or the 'Scriptures,' they are speaking of the Old Testament as we know it.

The Old Testament is not the end. It is Part One of a two part message from God. The New Testament completes the Old Testament.

Made in the USA
Middletown, DE
10 May 2024

54001477R00066